GW00750269

THE EVOLUTION OF CONSCIOUSNESS

THE EVOLUTION OF CONSCIOUSNESS

Rudolf Steiner

translated by
V. E. Watkin and C. Davy

published by

RUDOLF STEINER PRESS
LONDON

Previous Editions published by Rudolf Steiner Press, London.

First Edition in Pharos Books, London 1979.

Published in agreement with the Rudolf Steiner Nachlassverwaltung, Dornach, Switzerland.
Lectures given at Penmaenmawr, England, 19–31 August 1923. The German text is entitled *Initiations-Erkenntnis* (Vol. No. 227 in the *Bibliographical Survey*, 1961).

ISBN 0 85440 351 5

Made and printed in Great Britain by
The Garden City Press, Limited
Letchworth, Hertfordshire SG6 1JS

CONTENTS

I

First Steps towards Imaginative Knowledge

Throughout the ages, understanding the world has been closely associated with understanding man himself. It is generally recognised that in the days when not only material existence, but also spiritual life, was taken into consideration, man was looked upon as a microcosm, as a world in miniature. This means that man in his being and doing, in the whole part he plays in the world, was viewed as a concentration of all the laws and activities of the Cosmos. In those days it was insisted that understanding of the universe could be founded only on an understanding of man.

But here, for anyone who is unprejudiced, a difficulty arises at once. Directly he wants to arrive at so-called self-knowledge—the only true knowledge of man—he finds himself confronted by an overwhelming riddle; and after observing himself for a time, he is obliged to own that this being of his, as it appears in the world of the senses, is not completely revealed even to his own soul. He has to admit that for ordinary sense-perception part of his being remains hidden and unknown. Thus he is faced with the task of extending his self-knowledge, of thoroughly investigating his true being, before he can come to knowledge of the world.

A simple reflection will show that a man's true being, his inner activity as an individual, cannot be found in the world that holds good for his senses. For directly he passes through the gate of death, he is given over as a corpse to the laws and conditions of this sense-perceptible world. The laws of nature—those laws which prevail out there in the visible world—seize upon the physically dead man. Then that system of relationships, which we call the human organism, comes to an end; then, after a time depending upon the manner of his disposal, the physical man disintegrates.

From this simple reflection, therefore, we see that the sum of nature's laws, in so far as we come to know them through sense-observation, is adapted solely to breaking down the human organism and does nothing to build it up. So we have to look for those laws, for that other activity, which, during earthly life, from birth or conception to death, fight against the forces, the laws, of dissolution. In every moment of our life we are engaged with our true inward being in a battle with death.

If now we look round at the only part of the sense-world understood by people today, the mineral, lifeless world, this certainly is subject to the forces that signify death for the human being. It is pure illusion for natural scientists to think they could ever succeed, by relying on the laws of the external sense-world, in understanding even the plants. That will never be so. They will go some little way towards this understanding and may cherish it as an ideal, but it will never be possible really to fathom the plant—let alone the animal and physical man himself—with the aid of the laws which belong to the external world perceived by man.

As earthly beings, between conception and death, in our true inner being we are fighters against the laws of nature. And if we really want to rise to self-knowledge, we have to examine that activity in the human being which works against death. Indeed, if we are to investigate thoroughly man's being —which is our intention in these lectures—we shall have to show how, through a man's earthly development, it comes about that his inner activities ultimately succumb to death— how death gains the victory over the hidden forces opposing it.

All this is intended to show the course our studies are meant to take. For the truth of what I am now saying will be revealed only gradually in the various lectures. To begin with, therefore, we can merely indicate, by observing man without prejudice, where we have to look for his innermost being, for his personality, his individuality. This is not to be found within the realm of natural forces, but outside it.

There is, however, another indication—and such indications

are all I want to give to-day—that as earthly men we live always in the present moment. Here, too, we need only be sufficiently unprejudiced to grasp all that this statement implies. When we see, hear, or otherwise perceive through our senses, it is the actual moment that is all-important for us. Whatever has to do with the past or the future can make no impression on our ears, our eyes, or on any other sense. We are given up to the moment, and thereby to space.

But what would a man become were he entirely given up to the present moment and to space? By observing ordinary life around us we have ample proof that, if a man is thus completely engrossed, he is no longer man in the full sense. Records of illness give evidence of this. Well-authenticated cases can be quoted of persons who, at a certain time in their lives, become unable to remember any of their former experiences, and are conscious only of the immediate present. Then they do the craziest things. Contrary to their ordinary habits, they buy a railway ticket and travel to some place or other, doing everything necessary at the time quite sensibly, with more intelligence, and perhaps with more cunning, than usual. They have meals and do all the other little things in life at the normal time. On arrival at the station to which they booked, they take another ticket, going possibly in an opposite direction. They wander about in this way, it may be for years, until they come to a stop at some place, suddenly realising they don't know where they are. Everything they have done, from the moment they took the first ticket, or left their home, is blotted out from their consciousness, and they remember only what took place before that. Their life of soul, the whole of their life as human beings on earth, becomes chaotic. They no longer feel themselves to be a unified person. They had always lived in the present moment and had been able to find their way about in space, but now they have lost their inner feeling for time; they have lost their memory.

When a man loses his inner feeling for time—his really intimate connection with the past—then his life becomes a chaos. Experience of space alone can do nothing to help towards the health of his whole being.

To put this in other words: A man in his sense-life is always given up to the moment, and in some cases of illness it is possible for him to detach his immediate existence in space from his existence as a whole—but he is then no longer man in the full sense.

Here we have an indication of something in man belonging not to space but only to *time;* and we must say that if one human experience is that of space, there is also another which must always be present in a man—the experience of time. For him to remain man in the full sense, memory must make the past present in him. Being present in time is something indispensable for a man. Past time, however, is never there in the present moment; to experience it we must always carry it over into the present. Therefore in a human being there must be forces for conserving the past, forces that do not arise out of space and are therefore not to be understood as laws of nature working spatially, for they are outside space.

These indications point to the fact that if a man is to be the central point of knowledge of the world and has to begin by knowing himself, he must seek first of all within his own being for that which can raise him above spatial existence—the sole existence of which the senses tell—and can make him a being of time in the midst of his spatial existence. Therefore, if he is to perceive his own being, he must summon up from within himself cognitional powers which are not bound up with his senses or his perception of space. It is at this particular stage of human evolution, when natural science is having so momentous an effort in focussing attention on the laws of space, that, for reasons to be shown in these lectures, the true being of man has in general been entirely lost to view. Hence it is particularly necessary now to point out the inner experiences which, as you have seen, lead a man out of space into time and its experiences. We shall see how, going on from there, he actually enters the spiritual world.

The knowledge leading over from the world of the senses to the supersensible has been called, throughout the ages,

Initiation-knowledge—knowledge, that is, of what constitutes the true impulse, the active element, of human personality. It is of this Initiation-knowledge that I have to speak in these lectures, as far as is possible today. For our intention is to study the evolution of the world and of man, in the past, present and future, in the light of Initiation-knowledge.

I shall therefore have to begin by speaking of how such Initiation-knowledge can be acquired. The very way in which these matters are spoken of to-day clearly distinguishes present Initiation-knowledge from that of the past. In the past, individual teachers wrestled their way through to a perception of the supersensible in the world and in man. On the feelings of the students who came to them they made a strong impression by dint of their purely human qualities, and the students accepted the knowledge they offered, not under any compulsion, but in response to the teacher's personal authority.

Hence, for the whole of man's evolution up to the present time, you will always find described how there were separate groups of pupils, each under the guidance of a teacher, a "guru", to whose authority they submitted. Even on this point —as on many others we shall come across in these lectures— Initiation-knowledge to-day cannot follow the old path. The "guru" never spoke of the path by which he had achieved his own knowledge, and in those bygone times public instruction about the road to higher knowledge was never even considered. Such studies were pursued solely in the Mystery-centres which in those days served as universities for those following a supersensible path.

In the view of the general level of human consciousness which has been reached at this moment in history, such a path would no longer be possible. Anyone speaking of supersensible knowledge to-day is therefore naturally expected to say at once how this knowledge is to be acquired. At the same time everyone must be left free to decide, in accordance with his own way of life, his attitude to those exercises for body, soul and spirit, through which certain forces within man are developed. These forces look beyond the laws of nature, beyond the present moment, into the true being of the world, and therewith into the true being of man himself. Hence the obvious course for our studies is to begin with at least a few preliminary remarks about the way by which a man to-day can acquire knowledge of the supersensible.

We must thus take our start from man as he really is in earthly existence, in relation to space and the present moment. As an earthly being a man embraces in his soul and bodily nature—I say deliberately soul and bodily nature—a triad : a thinking being, a feeling being and a being of will. And when we look at everything that lies in the realm of thinking, in the realm of feeling and in that of the will, we have seen all of the human being that takes part in earthly existence.

Let us look first at the most important factor in man through which he takes his place in earthly existence. This is certainly his thinking. To his thinking nature he owes the clear-headedness he needs, as earthly man, for surveying the world. In comparison with this lucid thinking, his feeling is obscure, and, as for his willing—those depths of his being from which the will surges up—all that, for ordinary observation, is entirely out of range.

Just think how small a part your will plays in the ordinary world and in ordinary experience. Say you make up your mind to move a chair. You first have the thought of carrying it from one spot to another. You have a concept of this. The concept then passes, in a way you know nothing of, right into your blood and muscles. And what goes on in your blood and muscles—and also in your nerves—while you are lifting the chair and carrying it elsewhere, exists for you only as an idea. The real inner activity that goes on within your skin—of that you are wholly unconscious. Only the result comes into your thought.

Thus, of all your activities when awake, the will is the most unconscious. We will speak later of activity during sleep. During waking activity the will remains in absolute obscurity; a person knows as little about the passing of his thought into willing as in ordinary life on Earth he knows of what happens between falling asleep and waking. Even when anyone is awake, he is asleep where the inner nature of the will is concerned. It is only the faculty of forming concepts, of thinking, that enters clearly into man's life on Earth. Feeling lies midway between thinking and willing. And just as the dream stands between sleeping and waking, as an indefinite, chaotic conception, half-asleep, half-awake, so, coming halfway between willing and thinking, feeling is really a waking dream of the soul. We must take the clarity of thinking as our starting-point; but how does thinking run its course in ordinary life on Earth?

In the whole life of a human being on Earth, thinking plays a quite passive rôle. Let us be perfectly honest about this when observing ourselves. From the moment of waking until going to sleep a man is preoccupied with the affairs of the outer world. He lets sense-impressions flow into him, and with them concepts are then united. When sense-impressions pass away, only representations of them remain in the soul, turning gradually into memories. But, as I have said, if as earthly beings we observe ourselves honestly, we must admit that in concepts gained from ordinary life there is nothing which has not come into the soul from the external world through the senses. If without prejudice we examine what we carry deep down in our souls, we shall always find it was occasioned by some impression from without.

This applies particularly to the illusions of those mystics who—I am saying this expressly—do not penetrate to any great depth. They believe that by means of a more or less nebulous spiritual training they can come to an inward experience of a higher divinity underlying the world. And these mystics, these half or quarter mystics, are often heard to say how an inner light of the soul has dawned within them, how they have had some kind of spiritual vision.

Anyone who observes himself closely and honestly will come to see that many mystical visions can be traced to merely external sense-experiences which have been transformed in the course of time. Strange as it may seem, it is possible for some mystic, at the age perhaps of forty, to think he has had a direct, imaginative impression, a vision, of—we will take something concrete—the Mystery of Golgotha, that he sees the Mystery of Golgotha inwardly, spiritually. This gives him a feeling of great exaltation. Now a really good psychologist, who can go back through this mystic's earthly life, may find that as a boy of ten he was taken by his father on a visit, where he saw a certain little picture. It was a picture of the Mystery of Golgotha, and at the time it made hardly any impression on his soul. But the impression remained, and in a changed form sank deep down into his soul, to rise up in his fortieth year as a great mystical experience.

This is something to be stressed particularly when anyone ventures, more or less publicly, to say anything about the paths to supersensible knowledge. Those who do not take the matter very seriously generally talk in a superficial way. It is just those who wish to have the right to speak about mystical, supersensible paths who ought to know about the errors in this sphere which can lead people astray. They ought fully to realise that ordinary self-knowledge is chiefly made up of transformed external impressions, and that genuine self-knowledge must be sought to-day through inner development, by calling up forces in the soul not previously there. This requires us to realise the passive nature of our usual thinking. It deals with all impressions in the way natural to the senses. The earlier things come first, the later ones later; what is uppermost in thought remains above; what is below remains below. As a rule, therefore—not only in ordinary life but also in science—a man's concepts merely trail after processes in the external world. Our science has gone so far as to make an ideal of discovering how things run their course in the external world without letting thinking have the slightest influence on them. In their own sphere the scientists are quite right; by following this method they have made enormous advances. But they are more and more losing sight of man's true being. For the first step in those methods for developing inner forces of the soul leading to supersensible cognition, called by us meditation and concentration, is by finding the way over from purely passive thinking to thinking that is inwardly active.

I will begin by describing this first step in a quite elementary way. Instead of a concept aroused by something external, we can take a concept drawn entirely from within and give it the central place in our consciousness. What is important is not that the concept should correspond to a reality, but that it should be drawn up out of the depths of the soul as something active. Hence it is not good to take anything we remember, for in memory all manner of vague impressions cling to our concepts. If, therefore, we draw upon our memory we shall neither be sure that we are not letting extraneous things creep in, nor sure that we have really set about meditating with proper inward activity. There are three possible ways of proceeding, and there need be no loss of independence on any of them. A simple, easily apprehended concept is preferable, a creation of the moment, not having anything to do with what is remembered. For our purpose it can even be something quite paradoxical, deliberately removed from any passively received idea. We have only to make sure that the meditation has been brought about through our own inner activity.

The second way is to go to someone with experience in this sphere and ask him to suggest a subject for meditation. There may then be fear of becoming dependent on him. If, however, from the moment the meditation is received, one is conscious that every step has been taken independently, through an inner activity of one's own, and that the only thing not determined by oneself is the subject, which, since it comes from someone else, has to be actively laid hold of—when one is conscious of all this, there is no longer any question of dependence. It is then particularly necessary to continue to act in full consciousness.

And finally, the third way. Instruction can be sought from a teacher who—one might say—remains invisible. The student takes a book he has never seen before, opens it at random and reads any chance sentence. He can thus be sure of coming on something entirely new to him, and then he must work on it with inner activity. A subject for meditation can be made of the sentence, or perhaps of some illustration or diagram in the book, so long as he is certain he has never previously come across it. That is the third method, and in this way a teacher can be created out of nothing. The book has to be found and looked at, and a sentence, a drawing, or anything else chosen from it—all this constitutes the teacher.

Hence it is perfectly possible nowadays to take the path to higher knowledge in such a way that the active thinking required will not be unjustifiably encroached on by any other power. This is essential for present-day mankind. In the course of these lectures we shall see how necessary it is for people to-day, especially when they wish to make progress on the path to higher worlds, to respect and treasure their own free will. For how, otherwise, is any inner activity to be developed? Directly anyone becomes dependent on someone else, his own will is frustrated. And it is important that meditation to-day should be carried through with inner activity, out of the will in thinking, which is hardly at all valued to-day, with modern science putting all the emphasis on passive observation of the outer world.

In this way we can win through to active thinking, the rate of progress depending wholly on the individual. One man will get there in three weeks, if he perseveres with the same exercises. Another will take five years, another seven, and some-one else nineteen, and so on. The essential point is that he should never relax his efforts. A moment will come when he recognises that his thinking has really changed : it no longer runs on in the old passive pictures but is inwardly full of energy—a force which, although he experiences it quite clearly, he knows to be just as much a force as the force required to raise an arm or point a finger. We come to know a thinking that seems to sustain our whole being, a thinking that can hit against an obstacle. This is no figure of speech, but a concrete truth that we can experience. We know that ordinary thinking does no such thing. When I run up against a wall and get hurt, my physical body has received a blow through force of contact. This force of contact depends on my being able to hit my body against objects. It is I who do the hitting. The ordinary passive thinking does not hit any-thing, but simply presents itself to be hit, for it has no reality;

it is only a picture. But the thinking to which we come in the way described is a reality, something in which we live. It can hit against something as a finger can hit the wall. And just as we know that our finger cannot go through the wall, so we know that with this real thinking we cannot fathom everything. It is a first step. We have to take this step, this turning of one's own active thinking into an organ of touch for the soul, so that we may feel ourselves thinking in the same way that we walk, grasp or touch; so that we know we are living in a real being, not just in ordinary thinking which merely creates images, but in a reality, in the soul's organ of touch which we ourselves have become.

That is the first step—to change our thinking so that we feel: Now you yourself have become the thinker. That rounds off everything. With this thinking it is not the same as with physical touch. An arm, for instance, grows as we grow, so that when we are full-grown our proportions remain correct. But the thinking that has become active is like a snail—able to extend feelers or to draw them in again. In this thinking we live in a being certainly full of force but inwardly mobile, moving backwards and forwards, inwardly active. With this far-reaching organ of touch we can—as we shall see—feel about in the spiritual world; or, if this is spiritually painful, draw back.

All this must certainly be taken seriously by those with any desire to approach the true being of man—this transformation of one's whole nature. For we do not discover what a man actually is unless we start by seeing in him something beyond what is perceived by our earthly senses. All that is developed through the activity of thinking is a man's first supersensible member—later I shall be describing it more fully. First we have man's physical body that can be perceived by our ordinary sense-organs, and this offers resistance on meeting the ordinary organs of touch. Then we have our first supersensible member—we can call it the etheric body or the formative forces body. It must be called something, but the name is immaterial. In future I will call it the etheric or formative forces body. Here we have our first supersensible member, just as perceptible for a higher power of touching, into which thinking has been changed, as physical things are perceptible to the physical sense of touch. Thinking becomes a supersensible touching, and through this supersensible touching the etheric or formative forces body can be, in the higher sense, both grasped and seen. This is the first real step, as it were, into the supersensible world.

From the very way in which I have tried to describe the passing over of thinking into the experience of an actual force within one, you will realise how little sense there is, where genuine spiritual development is concerned, in saying, for example, that anyone who wishes to enter the spiritual world by this path is merely indulging in fantasy or yielding to auto-suggestion. For it is the first reaction of many people to say : "Anyone who talks of the higher worlds in connection with a training of this kind is simply picturing what he has suggested to himself." Then others take up the refrain, perhaps saying : "It is even possible that someone who loves lemonade has only to think of it and his mouth immediately begins to water, just as though he were drinking lemonade. Auto-suggestion has such power !"

All this may certainly be so, and anyone who is taking the rightful path we have indicated into the spiritual world must be well up in the things that physiologists and psychologists can get to know intellectually, and he should have a thoroughly practical acquaintance with the precautions that have to be observed. But to anyone who believes he can persuade himself by auto-suggestion that he is drinking lemonade, although he has none, I would reply : "Yes, that is possible —but show me the man who has quenched a real thirst with imaginary, auto-suggested lemonade !" That is where the difference begins between what is merely imagined passively and what is actually experienced. By keeping in touch with the real world and making our thinking active, we reach the stage of living spiritually in the world in such a way that thinking develops into a touching. Naturally it is a touching that has nothing to do with chairs or tables; but we learn to touch in the spiritual world, to make contact with it, to enter into a living relation with it. It is precisely by means of this active thinking that we learn to distinguish between the mystical fancies of auto-suggestion and the experience of spiritual reality.

All these objections arise from people not having yet looked into the way modern Initiation-knowledge describes the path for to-day. They are content to judge from outside a matter of which they may have heard simply the name, or of which they have gained a little superficial knowledge. Those who enter the spiritual world in the way here described, which enables them to make contact with it and to touch it, know how to distinguish between merely forming a subsequent concept of what they have experienced through active thinking and the perceptive experience itself. In ordinary life we can quite well distinguish between the experience of inadvertently burning our finger and a picturing of the incident afterwards! There is a most convincing difference, for in one case the finger is actually painful, in the other it is painful only in imagination. The same difference is encountered on a higher level between ideas we have of the spiritual world and what we actually experience there.

Now the first thing attained in this way is true self-knowledge. For, just as in life we have for our immediate perception a table here, chairs over there, and this whole splendid hall—with the clock that isn't going!—and so on; just as all this stands before us in space, and we perceive it at any moment, so, to the thinking that has become active and real, the world of time makes itself known—at first in the form of the time-world that is bound up with the human being himself. Past experiences that can normally be recovered only as memory-images stand before him as an immediately present tableau of long past events. The same thing is described by people who experience a shock through the threat of imminent death by drowning perhaps; and what they describe is confirmed—I always add this—by persons who think in an entirely materialistic way. To someone in mortal peril there may flash up an inward tableau of his past life. And this in fact is what happens also to people who have made their thinking active; suddenly before their souls arises a tableau of their life from the moment when they first learnt to think up to the present. Time becomes space; the past becomes present; a picture stands before their souls. The most characteristic feature of this experience—I shall have to go into it more closely to-morrow—is that, because the whole thing is like a picture, one still has a certain feeling of space, but only a *feeling*. For the space now experienced lacks the third dimension; it is two-dimensional only, as with a picture. For this reason I call this cognition Imaginative—a picture-cognition that works, as in a painting, with two dimensions.

You may ask : When I have this experience of only two dimensions, what happens if, still experiencing two dimensions, I go further? That makes no difference. We lose all experience of a third dimension. On a later occasion I will speak of how, in our day, because there is no longer any consciousness of such things, people searching for the spiritual look for a fourth dimension as a way towards it. The truth is that when we go on from the physical to the spiritual, no fourth dimension appears, but the third dimension drops away. We must get used to the real facts in this sphere, as we have had to do in others. It was once thought that the earth was flat, and ran off into an indefinite region where it came to an abrupt end; and just as it was an advance when people knew that if we sail round the earth we come back to our starting-point, so it will be an advance in our inner comprehension of the world when we know that, in the spiritual world, we do not go on from first, second, third dimensions to a fourth, but back to two dimensions only. And we shall see how, eventually, we go back to only one. That is the true state of affairs.

We can see how, in observing the outer world, people to-day cling in a superficial way to numbers : first dimension, second, third—and so a fourth must follow. No, we turn back to two dimensions; the third dissolves and we arrive at a truly

Imaginative-knowledge. It comes to us first as a tableau of our life, when we survey in mighty pictures the experiences of our past earthly life and how we have inwardly gone through them. And this differs considerably from simple memories.

Ordinary memory-pictures make us feel that they come essentially from conceptions of the outside world, experiences of pleasure, pain, of what other people have done to us, of their attitude towards us. That is what we chiefly experience in our purely conceptual memories.

In the tableau of which I am speaking, it is different. There we experience—well, let us take an example. Perhaps we met someone ten years ago. In ordinary memory we would see how he came to meet us, what he did to us that was good or bad, and so on. But in the life-tableau we re-live our first sight of the man, what we did and experienced ourselves in order to gain his friendship, what our impressions were. Thus in the tableau we feel what unfolds outwardly from within us, whereas ordinary memory shows what develops inwardly from without.

So of the tableau we can say that it brings us something like a present experience in which one thing does not follow another, as in recollection, but one thing is side-by-side with another in two-dimensional space. Hence the life-tableau can be readily distinguished from memory-pictures.

Now what is gained from this is an enhancement of our inner activity, the active experience of one's own personality. That is the essential feature of it. One lives in and develops more intensively the forces which radiate from the personality. Having gone through this experience, we have to climb a further step, and this is something that nobody does at all willingly. It entails the most rigorous inner discipline. For what is experienced through this life-tableau, through the pictures presenting one's own experiences to the soul, gives us, even in the case of past experiences that were actually painful, a feeling of personal happiness. A tremendously strong feeling of happiness is united with this Imaginative knowledge.

It is this subjective feeling of happiness which has inspired all those religious ideals and descriptions—in Mohammedanism, for instance—where life beyond the Earth is pictured in such glowing terms. They are an Imaginative result of this experience of happiness.

If the next step is to be made, this feeling of happiness must be forgotten. For when in perfect freedom we have first exerted our will to make our thinking active through meditation and concentration, as I have described, and by means of this active thinking we have advanced to experience of the life-tableau, we have then to use all our strength in blotting this out from our consciousness. In ordinary life this blotting out is often all too easy. Those who go in for examinations have good reason to complain of it! Ordinary sleep, too, is finally nothing but a passive wiping out of everything in our daytime consciousness. For the examination candidate would hardly wipe out his knowledge consciously; it is a passive process, a sign of weakness in one's command of present events. When, however, the required strength has been gained, this wiping out is necessary for the next step towards supersensible knowledge.

Now it easily happens that, by concentrating all the forces of his soul on a subject he himself has chosen, a man develops a desire to cling to it, and because a feeling of happiness is connected with this life-tableau, he clings to it all the more readily and firmly. But one must be able to extinguish from consciousness the very thing one has striven for through the enhancement of one's powers. As I have pointed out, this is much more difficult than the blotting out of anything in ordinary life.

You will no doubt be aware that when a person's sense-impressions have been gradually shut off; when all is dark around him and he can see nothing; when all noise is shut out so that he hears nothing and even the day's impressions are suppressed, he falls asleep. This empty consciousness, that comes to anyone on the verge of sleep, now has to be brought about at will. But while all conscious impressions, even those self-induced, have to be blotted out, it is most important for the student to remain awake. He must have the strength, the inner activity, to keep awake while no longer receiving impressions from without, or any experiences whatever. An empty consciousness is thus produced, but an empty consciousness of which one is fully aware.

When all that has been first brought to consciousness through enhanced forces has been wiped out and the consciousness made empty, it does not remain so, for then the second stage of knowledge is entered. In contrast to Imaginative knowledge, we may call it Inspired knowledge. If we have striven for empty consciousness by preparation of this kind—then, just as the visible world is normally there for our eyes to see and the world of sound for our ears to hear—it becomes possible for the spiritual world to present itself to our soul. It is no longer our own experiences, but a spiritual world that presses in on us. And if we are so strong that we have been able to suppress the entire life-tableau all at once—letting it appear and then blotting it out, so that after experiencing it we empty our consciousness of it—than the first perception to arise in this emptiness is of our pre-earthly life—the life before conception and descent into a physical body. This is the first real supersensible experience that comes to a man after he has emptied his consciousness—he looks at his own pre-earthly life. From that moment he comes to know the side of immortality which is never brought out to-day. People talk of immortality only as the negation of death. Certainly this side of immortality is as important as the other —we shall have much more to say about it—but the immortality we first come to know in the way I have briefly indicated is not the negation of death, but "unbornness", the negation of birth; and both sides are equally real. Only when people come once more to understand that eternity has these two sides—immortality and "unbornness"—will they be able to recognise again in man that which is enduring, truly eternal.

Modern languages all have a word for immortality, but they have lost the word "unbornness", although older languages had it. This side of eternity, "unbornness", was lost first, and now, in this materialistic age, the tragic moment is threatening when all knowledge of immortality may be lost—for in the realm of pure materialism people are no longer willing to know anything whatever of the spiritual part of man.

To-day I have been able to indicate—and quite briefly—only the very first steps on the path to supersensible worlds. During the next few days something further will be described, and then we shall turn back to what can be known on that path about man and the world, in the present and past, and also to what needs to be known for the future.

II

Inspiration and Intuition

Let us once more call up before our souls whither modern
Initiation leads, after the first steps to Imaginative knowledge
have been successfully taken. A man then comes to the point
where his previous abstract, purely ideal world of thought is
permeated with inner life. The thoughts coming to him are
no longer lifeless, passively acquired; they are an inward
world of living force which he feels in the same way as he
feels the pulsing of his blood or the streaming in and out of
the air he breathes. It is therefore a question of the ideal
element in thinking being replaced by an inward experience
of reality. Then indeed the pictures that previously constituted a man's thoughts are no longer mere abstract, shadowy
projections of the outside world, but are teeming with an
inward, vivid existence. They are real Imaginations experienced in two dimensions, as indicated yesterday, but it is not as
though a man were standing in front of a painting in the
physical world, for then he may experience visions, not
Imaginations. Rather is it as though, having lost the third
dimension, he were himself moving about within the picture.
Hence it is not like seeing something in the physical world;
anything that has the look of the physical world will be a
vision. Genuine Imagination comes to us only when, for example, we no longer *see* colours as we do in the physical
world, but when we *experience* them. What does this mean?

When you see colours in the physical world, they give you
different experiences. You perceive red as something that
attacks you, that wants to spring at you. A bull will react
violently to this aggressive red; he experiences it far more
vividly than does man, in whom the whole experience is
toned down.

When you perceive green, it gives you a feeling of balance, an experience neither painful nor particularly pleasant;

whereas blue induces a mood of devotion and humility. If we allow these various experiences of colour to penetrate right into us, we can realise how it is that when anything in the spiritual world comes at us in the aggressive way red does in physical life, it is something corresponding to the colour red. When we encounter something which calls up a mood of humility, this has the same effect as the experience of blue or blue-violet in the physical world. We can simplify this by saying : we have experienced red or blue in the spiritual world. Otherwise, for the sake of precision, we should always have to say : we have experienced something there in the way that red, or blue, is experienced in the physical world. To avoid so many words, one says simply that one has seen auric colours which can be distinguished as red, blue, green, and so on.

But we must realise thoroughly that this making our way into the supersensible, this setting aside of all that comes to us through the senses, is always present as a concrete experience. And in the course of this experience we always have the feeling I described yesterday, as if thinking had become an organ of touch extending throughout the human organism, so that spiritually we feel that a new world is opening out and we are touching it. This is not yet the real spiritual world, but what I might call the etheric or formative-forces world. Anyone who would learn to know the etheric must grasp it in this way. For no speculation, no abstract reflection, about the etheric can lead to true knowledge of it. In this thinking that has become real we live with our own formative-forces or etheric body, but it is a different kind of living from life in the physical body. I should like to describe this other way by means of a comparison.

When you look at one of your fingers, you recognise it as a living member of your organism. Cut it off, and it is no longer what it was; it dies. If this finger of yours had a consciousness, it would say : I am no more than a part of your organism, I have no independent existence. That is what a man has to say directly he enters the etheric world with Imaginative cognition. He no longer feels himself as a separate being, but as a member of the whole etheric world, the whole etheric cosmos. After that he realises that it is only by having a physical body that he becomes a personality, an individuality. It is the physical body that individualises and makes of one a separate being.

We shall indeed see how even in the spiritual world we can be individualised—but I will speak of that later. If we enter the spiritual world in the way described, we are bound at first to feel ourself as just one member of the whole etheric Cosmos; and if our etheric body were to be cut off from the cosmic ether, it would mean for us etheric death. It is very important to grasp this, so that we may understand properly what has to be said later about a man's passage through the gate of death.

As I pointed out yesterday, this Imaginative experience in the etheric, which becomes a tableau of our whole life from birth up to the present moment of our existence on Earth, is accompanied by an extraordinarily intense feeling of happiness. And the flooding of the whole picture-world by this inward, wonderfully pleasurable feeling is a man's first higher experience.

We must then be able—as I also mentioned yesterday— to take all we have striven for through Imagination, through our life-tableau, and make it all disappear at will. It is only when we have thus emptied our consciousness that we understand how matters really are in the spiritual world. For then we know that what we have seen up to now was not the spiritual world, but merely an Imaginative picture of it. It is only at this stage of empty consciousness that—just as the physical world streams into us through our senses—so the spiritual world streams into us through our thinking. Here begins our first real experience, our first real knowledge, of the objective spiritual world. The life-tableau was only of our own inner world. Imaginative cognition reveals only this inner world, which appears to higher knowledge as a picture-world, a world of cosmic pictures. The Cosmos itself, together with our own true being, as it was before birth, before our earthly existence, appear first at the stage of Inspiration, when the spiritual world flows into us from outside. But when we have arrived at being able to empty our consciousness, our whole soul becomes awake; and in this stage of pure wakefulness we must be able to acquire a certain inner stillness and peace. This peace I can describe only in the following way.

Let us imagine we are in a very noisy city and hear the roar of it all around us. This is terrible—we say—when, from all sides, tumult assails our ears. Suppose it to be some great modern city, such as London. But now suppose we leave this city, and gradually, with every step we take as we walk away, it becomes quieter and quieter. Let us imagine vividly this fading away of noise. Stiller and stiller it becomes. Finally we come perhaps to a wood where all is perfectly silent; we have reached the zero-point where nothing can be heard.

Yet we can go even further. To illustrate how this can happen, I will use a quite trivial comparison. Suppose we have in our purse a certain sum of money. As we spend it from day to day, it dwindles, just as the noise dwindles as we leave the town. At length comes the day when there is nothing left—the purse is empty. We can compare this nothingness with the silence. But what do we do next if we are not to grow hungry? We get into debt. I am not recommending this; it is meant only as a comparison. How much have we then in our purse? Less than nothing; and the greater the debt, the more we have less than nothing.

And now let us imagine it to be the same with this silence. There would be not only the absolute peace of the zero-point of silence, but it would go further and come to the negative of hearing, quieter than quiet, more silent than silence. And this must in fact happen when, in the way described yesterday, we are able through enhanced powers to reach this inner peace and silence. When, however, we arrive at this inner negative of audibility, at this peace greater than the zero-point of peace, we are then so deeply in the spiritual world that we not only see it but hear it resounding. The world of pictures becomes a world of resounding life; and then we are in the midst of the true spiritual world. During the moments we spend there we are standing, as it were, on the shore of existence; the ordinary sense-world vanishes, and we know ourselves to be in the spiritual world. Certainly—I will say more of this later—we must be properly prepared so that we are at all times able to return. But there is something else to come—an experience previously unknown. Directly this peace is achieved in the empty consciousness, what I have described as an inwardly experienced, all-embracing, cosmic feeling of happiness gives way to an equally all-embracing pain. We come to feel that the world is built on a foundation of cosmic suffering—of a cosmic element which can be experienced by the human being only as pain. We learn the penetrating truth, so willingly ignored by those who look outside themselves for happiness, that everything in existence has finally to be brought to birth in pain. And when, through Initiation-knowledge, this cosmic experience of pain has made its impression upon us, then out of real inner knowledge we can say the following :

If we study the human eye—the eye that reveals to us the beauty of the physical world, and is so important for us that through it we receive nine-tenths of the impressions that make up our life between birth and death—we find that the eye is embedded in a bodily cavity which originates from a wound. What was done originally to bring about the eye-sockets could be done to-day only by actually cutting out a hollow in the physical body. The ordinary account of evolution gives a much too colourless impression of this. These sockets into which the eyeballs were inserted from outside—as indeed the physical record of evolution shows—were hollowed out at a time when man was still an unconscious being. If he had been conscious of it, it would have involved a painful wounding of the organism.

Indeed, the whole human organism has been brought forth out of an element which for present-day consciousness would be an experience of pain. At this stage of knowledge we have a deep feeling that, just as the coming forth of the plants means pain for the Earth, so all happiness, everything in the world from which we derive pleasure and blessing, has its roots in an element of suffering. If as conscious beings we could suddenly be changed into the substance of the ground beneath our feet, the result would be an endless enhance-- ment of our feeling of pain.

When these facts revealed out of the spiritual world are put before superficially-minded people, they say : "My idea of God is quite different. I have always thought of God in His power as founding everything upon happiness, just as we would wish." Such people are like that King of Spain to whom someone was showing a model of the universe and the course of the stars. The King had the greatest difficulty in understanding how all these movements occurred, and finally he exclaimed : "If God had left it to me, I would have made a much simpler world."

Strictly speaking, that is the feeling of many people where knowledge and religion are concerned. Had God left the creation to them, they would have made a simpler world. They have no idea how naive this is !

Genuine Initiation-knowledge cannot merely satisfy men's desire for happiness; it has to guide them to a true under- standing of their own being and destiny as they come forth from the world in the past, present and future. For this, spiritual facts are necessary, instead of something which gives immediate pleasure. But there is another thing which these lectures should indeed bring out. Precisely by experienc- ing such facts, if only through knowing them conceptually, people will gain a good deal that satisfies an inward need for their life here on Earth. Yes, they will gain something they need in order to be human beings in the fullest sense, just as for completeness they need their physical limbs.

The world we meet in this way when we go on beyond Imagination into the stillness of existence, out of which the spiritual world reveals itself in colour and in sound—this world differs essentially from the world perceived by the senses. When we are living with it—and we have to live *with* the spiritual world when it is present for us—we see how all sense-perceptible, physical things and processes really proceed from out of the spiritual world. Hence as earthly men we see only one half of the world; the other half is occult, hidden from us. And through every opening, every happening, in the physical-material world, one might say, this hidden half reveals its spiritual nature first in the pictures of Imagination, and then through its own creative activity in Inspiration. In the world of Inspiration we can feel at home, for here we find the origins of all earthly things, all earthly creations. And here, as I have indicated, we discover our own pre-earthly existence.

Following an old image, I have called this world, lying beyond that of Imagination, the astral world—the name is not important—and what we bring along with us from that world, and have carried into our etheric and physical bodies, we may speak of as our astral body. In a certain sense, it encloses the Ego-organisation. For higher knowledge, accordingly, the human being consists of four members : physical body, etheric or formative-forces body, astral body, and Ego-organisation. Knowledge of the Ego, however, entails a further supersensible step, which in my book, *Knowledge of the Higher Worlds,* I have called "Intuition". The term Intuition may easily be misunderstood because, for example, anyone with imaginative, poetic gifts will often give the name of intuition to his sensitive feeling for the world. This kind of intuition is only a dim feeling; yet it has some relation to the Intuition of which I am speaking. For just as earthly man has his sense-perceptions, so in his feeling and his will he has a reflection of the highest kind of cognition, of Intuition. Otherwise he could not be a moral being. The dim promptings of conscience are a reflection, a kind of shadow-picture, of true Intuition, the highest form of cognition possible for man on Earth.

Earthly man has in him something of what is lowest, and also this shadow-picture of what is highest, accessible only through Intuition. It is the intermediate levels that are lacking in him; hence he has to acquire Imagination and Inspiration. He has also to acquire Intuition in its purity, in its light-filled inner quality. At present it is in his moral feeling, his moral conscience, that he possesses an earthly image of that which arises as Intuition. Hence we can say that when a man with Initiation-knowledge rises to actual Intuitive knowledge of the world, of which previously he has known only the natural laws, the world becomes as intimately connected with him on earth as only the moral world is now. And this is indeed a significant feature of human life on Earth—that out of a dim inner presentiment we connect with the highest realm of all something which, in its true form, is accessible only to enhanced cognition.

The third step in higher knowledge, necessary for rising to Intuition, can be achieved only by developing to its highest point a faculty which, in our materialistic age, is not recognised as a cognitional force. What is revealed through Intuition can be attained only by developing and spiritualising to the highest degree the capacity for love. A man must be able to make this capacity for love into a cognitional force. A good preparation for this is to free ourselves in a certain sense from dependence on external things; for instance, by making it our regular practice to picture our past experiences not in their usual sequence but in reverse order.

In ordinary passive thinking we may be said to accept world events in an altogether slavish way. As I said yesterday : In our very thought-pictures we keep the earlier as the earlier, the later as the later; and when we are watching the course of a play on the stage the first act comes first, then the second, and so on to a possible fifth. But if we can accustom ourselves to picture it all by beginning at the end and going from the fifth act back through the fourth, third, second, to the first, then we break away from the ordinary sequence—we go backwards instead of forwards. But that is not how things happen in the world : we have to strain every nerve to call up from within the force to picture events in reverse. By so doing we free the inner activity of our soul from its customary leading-strings, and we gradually enable the inner experiences of our soul and spirit to reach a point where soul and spirit break loose from the bodily and also from the etheric element. A man can well prepare himself for this breaking away if every evening he makes a backward survey of his experiences during the day, beginning with the last and moving back. When possible even the details should be conceived in a backward direction: if you have gone upstairs, picture yourself first on the top step, then on the step below it, and so on backwards down all the stairs.

You will probably say: "But there are so many hours during the day, full of experiences." Then first try taking episodes—picturing, for instance, this going up and down stairs in reverse. One thus acquires inner mobility, so that gradually one becomes able to go back in imagination through a whole day in three or four minutes.

But that, after all, is only the negative half of what is needed for enhancing and training spiritually our capacity for loving. This must be brought to the point when, for example, we lovingly follow each stage in the growth of a plant. In ordinary life this growth is seen only from outside—we do not take part in it. We must learn to enter into every detail of plant-growth, to dive right down into the plant, until in our own soul we become the plant, growing, blossoming, bringing forth fruit with it, and the plant becomes as dear to us as we are to ourselves. In the same way we can go above the plants to picture the life of animals, and down to the minerals. We can feel how the mineral forms itself into the crystal, and take inward pleasure in the shaping of its planes, corners, angles, and having a sensation as of pain in our own being when the minerals are split asunder. Then, in our souls, we enter not only with sympathy but with our will into every single event in nature.

All this must be preceded by a capacity for love extending to mankind as a whole. We shall never be able to love nature in the right way until we have first succeeded in loving all our fellow-men. When we have in this way won through to an understanding love for all nature, that which made itself perceptible first in the colours of the aura, and in the resounding of the spheres, rounds itself out and takes on the outlines of actual spiritual Beings.

Experiencing these spiritual Beings, however, is a different matter from experiencing physical things. When a physical object is in front of me, for example this clock, I stand here with the clock there, and can experience it only by looking at it from outside. My relation to it is determined by space. In this way one could never have any real experience of a spiritual Being. We can have it only by entering right into the spiritual Being, with the aid of the faculty for loving which we have cultivated first towards nature. Spiritual Intuition is possible only by applying—in stillness and emptiness of consciousness—the capacity for love we can first learn in the realm of nature. Imagine that you have developed this capacity for loving minerals, plants, animals and also man; you are now in the midst of a completely empty consciousness. All around is the peace which lies beyond its zero-point. You feel the suffering on which the whole existence of the world is founded, and this suffering is at the same time a loneliness. Nothing yet is there. But the capacity for love, flowing up from within in manifold forms, leads you on to enter with your own being into all that now appears visibly, audibly, as Inspiration. Through this capacity for love you enter first into one spiritual Being, then into another.

These Beings described in my book, *Occult Science,* these Beings of the higher Hierarchies—we now learn to live in our experience of them; they become for us the essential reality of the world. So we experience a concrete spiritual world, just as through eye and ear, through feeling and warmth, we experience a concrete physical world.

If anyone wishes to acquire knowledge particularly important for himself, he must have advanced to this stage. I have already mentioned that through Inspiration pre-earthly spiritual existence rises up in our soul; how in this way we learn what we were before we came down into an earthly body. When through the capacity for love we are able to enter clairvoyantly into spiritual Beings, in the way I have described, there is also revealed that which first makes a man, in his inner experience, a complete being. There is revealed what precedes our life in the spiritual world; we are shown what we were before ascending to the last spiritual life be-

tween death and rebirth. The preceding earthly life is revealed, and, one after another, the lives on Earth before
that. For the true Ego, present in all the repeated lives on
Earth, can manifest only when the faculty for love has been
so greatly enhanced that any other being, whether outside
in nature or in the spiritual world, has become just as dear
to a man as in his self-love he is dear to himself. But the true
Ego—the Ego that goes through all repeated births and deaths
—is manifest to a man only when he no longer lives
egotistically for momentary knowledge, but in a love that can
forget self-love and can live in an objective Being in the way
that in physical existence he lives in self-love. For this Ego of
former lives on Earth has then become as objective for his present life as a stone or a plant is for us when we stand outside
it. We must have learnt by then to comprehend in objective
love something which, for our present subjective personality,
has become quite objective, quite foreign. We must have
gained mastery over ourselves during our present earthly existence in order to have any insight into a preceding one.

When we have achieved this knowledge, we see the complete life of a man passing rhythmically through the stages of
earthly existence from birth or conception till death, and then
through spiritual stages between death and rebirth, and then
returning again to Earth, and so on. A complete earthly life
reveals itself as a repeated passing through birth and death,
with intermediate periods of life in purely spiritual worlds.
Only through Intuition can this knowledge be acquired as
real knowledge, derived directly from experience.

I have had to describe for you—in outline to begin with—
the path of Initiation-knowledge that must be followed in
our time, at this present stage of human evolution, in order to
arrive at true spiritual knowledge of the world and of man.
But as long as human beings have existed there has been
Initiation-knowledge, although it has had to take various
forms in different evolutionary periods. As man is a being who
goes through each successive earthly life in a different way,

conditions for his inner development in the various epochs of world-evolution have to vary considerably. We shall be learning more about these variations in course of the next few days; to-day I should like to say only that the Initiation-knowledge which had to be given out in early times was very different from what has to be given out to-day. We can go back some thousands of years, to a time long before the Mystery of Golgotha, and we find how greatly men's attitude to both the natural world and the spiritual world differed from that of the present time, and how different, accordingly, was their Initiation-knowledge from what is appropriate to-day.

We have now a very highly developed natural science; I shall not be speaking of its most advanced side but only of what is imparted to children of six or seven, as general knowledge. At this comparatively early age a child has to accept the laws relating, let us say, to the Copernican world-system, and on this system are built hypotheses as to the origin of the universe. The Kant-Laplace theory is then put forward and, though this theory has been revised, yet in its essentials it still holds good. The theory is based on a primeval nebula, demonstrated in physics by an experiment intended to show the earliest conditions of the world-system. This primeval nebula can be imitated experimentally, and out of it, through the rotation of certain forces, the planets are assumed to have come into being, and the sun left behind. One of the rings split off from the nebula is thought to have condensed into the shape of the Earth, and everything else—minerals, plants, animals, and finally man himself—is supposed to have evolved on this basis. And all this is described in a thoroughly scientific way.

The process is made comprehensible for children by means of a practical demonstration which seems to show it very clearly. A drop of oil is taken, sufficiently fluid to float on a little water; this is placed on a piece of card where the line of the equator is supposed to come; a pin is run through the card and the card is whirled round. It can then be shown how, one after another, drops of oil detach themselves and rotate, and you can get a miniature planetary system out of the oil, with a sun left in the middle. When that has been shown to us in childhood, why should we think it impossible for our planetary system to have arisen out of the primeval nebula? With our own eyes we have seen the process reproduced.

Now in moral life it may be admirable for us to be able to forget ourselves, but in a demonstration of natural phenomena it is not so good! This whole affair of the drop of oil would never have worked if there had been no-one there to twirl the pin. That has to be taken into account. If this hypothesis is to hold good, a giant schoolmaster would have had to be there in the Cosmos, to start the primeval nebula revolving and keep it turning. Otherwise the idea has no reality.

It is characteristic of this materialistic age, however, to conceive only a fraction of the truth, a quarter, an eighth, or even less, and this fraction then lives with terribly suggestive power in the souls of men. Thus we persist to-day in seeing one side only of nature and of nature's laws.

I could give you plenty of examples, from different spheres of life, clearly showing this attitude towards nature : how— because a man absorbs this with the culture of the day—he considers nature to be governed by what is called the law of cause and effect. This colours the whole of human existence to-day. At best, a man can still maintain some connection with the spiritual world through religious tradition, but if he wishes to rise to the actual spiritual world, he must undertake an inner training through Imagination, Inspiration, Intuition— as I have pictured them. He must be led by Initiation-knowledge away from this belief in nature as permeated throughout by law, and towards a real grasp of the spiritual. Initiation-knowledge to-day must aim at leading men from the naturalistic interpretation of the Cosmos, now taken for granted, to a realisation of its spirituality.

In the old Initiation-knowledge, thousands of years ago, the very opposite prevailed. The wise men of the Mysteries, the

leaders in those centres which were school, church, and art-
school at the same time, had around them people who knew
nothing of nature in the Copernican sense, but in their soul
and spirit had an instinctive, intimate experience of the
Cosmos, expressed in their myths and legends, which in the
ordinary civilisation of to-day are no longer understood.
About this too we shall have more to say. The experience
that men had in those early days was instinctive; an experience of soul and spirit. It filled their waking hours with the
dreamlike pictures of imagination; and from these pictures
came the legends, the myths, the sayings of the gods, which
made up their life. A man looked out into the world, experiencing his dreamy imaginations; and at other times he
lived in the being of nature. He saw the rainbows, the clouds,
the stars, and the sun making its speedy way across the
heavens; he saw the rivers, the hills arising; he saw the
minerals, plants, animals.

For primeval man, everything he saw through his senses
was a great riddle. For at the time of which I am speaking,
some thousands of years before the Mystery of Golgotha—
there were both earlier and later times when civilisation was
different—a man had an inward feeling of being blessed when
dreamlike imaginations came to him. The external world of the
senses, where all that he perceived of rainbow, clouds, the
moving sun, and the minerals, plants, animals, was what
the eye could see, while in the starry world he saw only what
the pre-Copernican, Ptolemaic system recorded. This external
world presented itself to people generally in a way that led
them to say: "With my soul I am living in a divine-
spiritual world, but there outside is a nature forsaken by the
gods. When with my senses I look at a spring of water, I see
nothing spiritual there; I see nothing spiritual in the rainbow,
in the minerals, plants, animals, or in the physical bodies of
men." Nature appeared to these people as a whole world that
had fallen away from divine spirituality.

This was how people felt in that time when the whole
visible Cosmos had for them the appearance of having fallen
away from the divine. To connect these two experiences, the

inward experience of God and the outer one of a fallen sense-world, it was not merely abstract knowledge they needed, but a knowledge that could console them for belonging to this fallen sense-world with their physical bodies and their etheric bodies. They needed a consolation which would assure them that this fallen sense-world was related to all they experienced through their instinctive imaginings, through an experience of the spiritual which, though dim and dreamlike, was adequate for the conditions of those times. Knowledge had to be consoling.

It was consolation, too, that was sought by those who turned eagerly to the Mysteries, either to receive only what could be given out externally, or to become pupils of the men of wisdom who could initiate them into the secrets of existence and the riddles that confronted them.

These wise men of the old Mysteries, who were at the same time priests, teachers, and artists, made clear to their pupils through everything contained in their Mysteries—yet to be described—that even in this fallen world, in its rising springs, in the blossoming trees and flowers, in the crystal-forming minerals, in rainbow and drifting clouds and journeying sun there live those divine-spiritual powers which were experienced instinctively in the dreamlike imaginations of men. They showed these people how to reconcile the god-forsaken world with the divine world perceived in their imaginations. Through the Mysteries they gave them a consoling knowledge which enabled them once more to look on nature as filled with the divine.

Hence we learn from what is told of those past ages—told even of the Grecian age—that knowledge now taught to the youngest children in our schools, that the sun stands still and the earth circles around it, for instance, is the kind of knowledge which in the old Mysteries was preserved as occult. What with us is knowledge for everyone was for that age occult knowledge; and explanations of nature were an occult science. As anyone can see who follows the course of human development during our civilisation, nature and nature's laws are the chief concern of men today; and this has led the

spiritual world to withdraw. The old dreamlike imaginations have ceased. A man feels nature to be neutral, not entirely satisfying, belonging not to a fallen, sinful Universe, but
to a Cosmos that by reason of inner necessity has to be as it is.
He then feels more sharply conscious of himself; he learns to
find spirituality in that one point only, and he discovers an
inner urge to unite this inner self with God. All he now
needs—in addition to his knowledge of nature and in conformity with it—is that a new Initiation-knowledge shall
lead him into the spiritual world. The old Initiation-knowledge could start from the spirit, which was then experienced
by people instinctively, and, embodied in the myths, could
lead them on to nature. The new Initiation-knowledge must
begin with a man's immediate experience to-day, with his
perception of the laws of nature in which he believes, and
from there it must point the way back to the spiritual world
through Imagination, Inspiration, Intuition.

Thus, in human evolution, a few thousand years before
the Mystery of Golgotha, we see the significant moment of
time when men, starting out from an instinctive experience of
the spirit, found their way to concepts and ideas which, as the
most external form of occult science, included the laws of
nature. To-day these laws of nature are known to us from
childhood. In face of this indifferent, prosaic attitude to life,
this naturalism, the spiritual world has withdrawn from the
inner life of man. Today, Initiation-knowledge must point
back from nature to the spirit. For the men of old, nature
was in darkness, but the spirit was bright and clear. The old
Initiation-knowledge had to carry the light of this brightness
of the spirit into the darkness of nature, so that nature too
might be illumined. Initiation-knowledge to-day has to start
from the light thrown upon nature, in an external, naturalistic
way, by Copernicus, Giordano Bruno, Galileo, Kepler, Newton and others. This light has then to be rescued, given fresh
life, in order to open the way for it to the spirit, which in its
own light must be sought on the opposite path to that of the
old Initiation.

III

Initiation-Knowledge — New and Old

In the study of Anthroposophy, a justifiable objection at first can be that the anthroposophical investigation of facts concerning the spiritual worlds depends upon calling up, through the training I have described, deep-lying forces in the human being, before these facts can be reached. Hence it might be said : All those who have not gone through such a development, and have therefore not yet reached the point of perceiving supersensible facts for themselves, and actually experiencing supersensible beings, have no means of proving the truth of what is said by the investigator of those worlds. Often, when the spiritual world is spoken of in public and information about it is given, the protest is heard : How should such ideas concern those who cannot yet see into this supersensible world?

This objection rests on an entirely erroneous idea—the idea that anyone who speaks about the supersensible worlds is talking of things quite unknown to his listeners. That is not so at all. But there is an important distinction, with regard to this kind of Initiation-knowledge, between what is right to-day and what was once right in the old days of which I was speaking yesterday.

You will remember how I described the path into the spiritual worlds. I spoke of how it leads us first to a great life-tableau, in which we see the experiences that have become part of our personality during this life on Earth. I went on to speak of how, having progressed from Imaginative-knowledge to that of Inspiration, a man is able, with empty consciousness and in absolute stillness and peace, to survey his pre-earthly life. He is thus led into that world of spiritual deeds which he has passed through between his last death and his recent descent to Earth.

Consider how, before making this descent, every human

being has gone through such experiences; there is no-one who has not experienced in its full reality what the spiritual investigator has to tell. And when the investigator clothes in words facts at first unrecognised, he is not appealing to something quite unknown to his hearers but to what everyone has experienced before earthly life. The investigator of the spiritual world is simply evoking people's cosmic memories; and all that he says about the spiritual world is living in the souls of everyone, though in the transition from pre-earthly to earthly life it has been forgotten. In fact, as an investigator of the spiritual world, one is simply recalling to people's memories something they have forgotten.

Now imagine that during life on Earth a man comes across another human being with whom he remembers experiencing something, twenty years before, which the other man has completely forgotten. By talking with him, however, about the incident that he himself remembers clearly, he can bring the other man to recall it also. It is just the same process, though on a higher level, when I speak to you about spiritual worlds, the only difference being that pre-earthly experiences are more completely forgotten than those of earthly life. It is only because people are disinclined to ask themselves seriously whether they find anything in their souls in tune with what is said by the spiritual investigator—it is only because of this feeling of antipathy that they do not probe into their souls deeply enough when hearing or reading what the investigator relates. Hence this is thought to be something of which he alone has knowledge, something incapable of proof. But it can quite well be proved by those who throw off the prejudice arising from the antipathy referred to. For the spiritual investigator is only recalling what has been experienced by each one of us in pre-earthly existence.

Now someone might say: Why should anyone be asked, during his life on Earth, to take on this extra task of concerning himself with matters which, in accordance with cosmic ordering, or one might say with divine decree, he experiences during life beyond the Earth? There are those, too, who ask : Why should I go to this trouble before death to gain knowledge about the supersensible worlds? I can very well wait till I am dead. Then, if all these things really exist, I shall come face to face with them.

All this, however, arises from a misunderstanding of earthly life. The facts of which the spiritual investigator speaks are experienced by human beings in pre-earthly existence, but they are not then the subject of thought, and only during life on Earth can thoughts about them be experienced. And only those thoughts about the supersensible world that have been worked upon during earthly life can be carried with us through the gate of death, and only then can we understand the facts we experience between death and rebirth.

One might say—if one wished to give an uncompromising picture—that at this present stage of evolution a man's life after death is extraordinarily hard if, during life on Earth, he gives no thought to the spiritual world. For, having passed through the gate of death, he can no longer acquire any real knowledge of his surroundings. He is in the midst of what is incomprehensible for him. Understanding of what is experienced after death has to be striven for during life on Earth. You will learn from further descriptions that it was different for men of earlier ages. But, at the present moment of human evolution, men will be increasingly constrained to strive for an understanding of what they are to experience in the supersensible world between death and rebirth. So one can say that speaking publicly of Spiritual Science is fully justified, for it can be proved by everyone. When it is established deeply enough in a man's soul, he will gradually come to say to himself : "What has been said through this spiritual investigator lights things up for me. It is just as if I had already experienced it all, and was now being given the thoughts in which to clothe the experience." For this reason, when speaking of Spiritual Science, of spiritual knowledge, it is very necessary to choose terms of expression different from those used in ordinary life. The point is that a student of Spiritual Science, through the very words used, should have the impression : "I am learning something which does not hold good for the sense-world, something which in the sense-world is sheer nonsense."

Then, you see, our opponents come and say : "What is said there about spiritual knowledge is all nonsense—pure fancy." As long as these people know of nothing outside the world of the senses, and do not want to know of anything else, such a statement is justified, for the supersensible world looks different from that of the senses. But if someone forgoes the one-sided witness of his senses and delves more deeply into his own soul, then he will say : "What the spiritual investigator says should simply give me the impulse to draw up from my own soul what is already there."

Naturally there is much to hinder our making such a confession. Yet, where understanding of the supersensible worlds is concerned, it is the most necessary confession of all. And it will be found that even the most difficult things become comprehensible when we are willing to penetrate in this way into our own depths.

There is no doubt that mathematical truths are among the most difficult things. They are held to be irrefutable. But the curious fact is that on entering the spiritual world we find that our mathematics and geometry are no longer correct. A very simple example will make this clear. From early youth we have learnt to look upon the old truths of Euclid as axiomatic, self-evident. For instance, it is stated as obvious that, given two points, A and B, the shortest distance between them is a straight line, and that any curved path between them is longer.

On a recognition of this fact—obvious for the physical world—rests the greater part of our geometry. But in the spiritual world it is the other way round. The straight line there from A to B is the longest way, and any other way is shorter because it can be taken in freedom. If at the point A one thinks of going to B, this very idea suggests an indirect way; and to hold to a straight course, and so at each single point to keep in the same direction, is hardest and causes most delay. Hence, in determining the most direct way in the two-dimensional or one-dimensional space of the spiritual world, we look for the longest way.

Now anyone who reflects about attentiveness, and delves deeply into his soul to discover what attentiveness really means, will find that in this connection, also, what is said by the spiritual investigator is true. For he will say to himself : "When I go around just as I choose, I get there easily, and I don't have to worry about traversing a particular stretch; I need do only what I do every day." And most people are bustling around from morning to night. They are in such a hurry that they hardly notice how much of all they do is done from sheer habit—what they have done the day before, what other people say they should do, and so forth. Then it all goes smoothly. Just think what it would be like if you had to pay careful attention to every detail of what you do during the day. Try it ! You will soon see how this slows you down.

Now in the spiritual world nothing is done without attentiveness, for there is no such thing as habit. Moreover, there is no such word as the impersonal pronoun "one"—at a certain hour one must have lunch, or one must have dinner at some other time. This "one"—for this occasion one ought to dress in a certain way, and so on—all that under the aegis of this little word plays such a great part in the physical world, particularly in our present civilisation, has no place in the spiritual world. There, we have to follow with individual attention every smallest step, and even less than a step. This is expressed in the words : In the spiritual world the straight way between two points is the longest way. So we have this contrast : In the physical world the direct way between two points is the shortest, whereas the direct way between two points is the longest in the spiritual world.

If we go down far enough into our soul, we find we can draw up from its depths a real understanding of this curious circumstance; and it becomes easier and easier to admit : "What the spiritual investigator says is actually wisdom I myself possess—I have only to be reminded of it."

Then, side by side with this—since the steps to be taken for acquiring supersensible cognition can to-day be found in books such as *Knowledge of the Higher Worlds*—everyone, in so far as his destiny, his karma, make it possible, can, as we shall see, follow this path and thus acquire his own perception of the spiritual worlds. In this way he comes to knowledge of the facts. Understanding for the ideas of the spiritual world has to be won by his coming to know in his own being all that was forgotten on entering earthly life.

Now it may be said that anyone is capable of grasping knowledge of the spiritual world when it is communicated in ideas. Thus, for understanding what the spiritual investigator offers, all that a man needs is his own sound, unprejudiced reason, provided it searches deeply enough into the soul. The investigator of spiritual facts, entering into the spiritual world, and speaking of its facts from first-hand knowledge—all this naturally requires a person to have pursued the path of knowledge on his own account. Hence it is justifiable for anyone who has acquired knowledge of the spiritual worlds to speak of them quite publicly to-day; for what people now absorb in life, if only at school, is an intellectual capacity, a power of discrimination, which equips them to understand what Spiritual Science brings forward. Here, too, things were different in earlier times, and the teachers in the Mysteries, the teachers of art and religion, went about it in a different way. Anyone to-day who speaks about spiritual knowledge to his contemporaries must so order his ideas that memories are aroused of their pre-earthly life. What he says to his audience, what he writes for his readers, must be so arranged that memories of the life before birth are evoked.

Whenever one speaks about Spiritual Science it is as if this appeal were made to the audience : Listen to what is said, and if you look deeply enough into your souls you will find it all there. Moreover, it will dawn on you that you cannot have learnt it during your life on Earth; no flower, no cloud, no spring, nothing earthly can have told you, not even science—for that is founded on the senses and the intellect. Gradually you will realise that you have brought this knowledge with you into earthly life, and that before this life you took part in things which have lingered on in your soul as a cosmic memory. All this has ben stirred up in you by the spiritual investigator. What he says, therefore, is indeed a call to the very depths of the human soul, not a demand that you should accept anything unknown. It is simply an appeal to men to call up in memory the greatest treasures of their own souls.

It was not so for mankind in the distant past. The wise men of the Mysteries, the priests, had to proceed in another way, for people then had a spontaneous memory of their pre-earthly existence. A few thousand years ago, even the most primitive man would never have questioned the presence in his soul of something brought down with him from the super-sensible into the life of the senses; it was an everyday experience in his dreamlike imaginations. In his soul he had something of which he said: "I do not owe this to my eyes that see the trees; I do not hear it with my ears that listen to the nightingale's song; nor have I received it through any other sense. I cannot have absorbed it during life on Earth; it was there as I made my descent; and when as an embryo I was given my earthly, physical body by another human body, there was already within me that which lights up now in my dreamlike imaginations. I have clothed it in my physical human body."

Hence in those olden days a man would not have been shown the way to further development by his attention being called to what must be emphasised to-day: that we have a memory, at first unconscious but capable of being made conscious, of pre-earthly existence. In the old Mysteries, attention had to be drawn to something quite different.

A man in those days had a feeling of intense sadness when looking at all that was most lovely in the sense-world. He looked at the flowers, springing out of the earth in their wonderful beauty, and watched the blossoms unfold. And he saw also how beneficent the flowers were for him. He saw the loveliness of the springs bubbling forth in shady places, and his senses spoke to him of their refreshing powers. But then, then, he said to himself: "It seems as though all this has fallen—fallen through sin from the world I bear within me and which I have brought down into physical existence out of spiritual worlds." So the teachers in the Mysteries then had the task of explaining how in the flowers, in the rippling waters, in the woodland murmurings and the song of the nightingale—everywhere spirit is working and weaving, everywhere spiritual beings are to be found. They had to impart to men the great truth: What is living in you lives also outside in nature. For a man looked upon the external world with sorrow, with pain, at the very time when his senses were freshest and most responsive—a time when least of all the intellect spoke to him of natural laws, and he looked upon the outer world with primitive senses. The beauty of its sprouting and budding forced itself upon his sight, his hearing and other senses; but all he felt was sorrow; for he was unable to reconcile it with the content of his pre-natal existence, which still lived on in his soul. Thus it was incumbent upon the wise men of the Mysteries to point out how the divine-spiritual dwells in all things, even in those of the senses. It was the spirituality of nature that these teachers had to make clear.

This, however, could be done only by taking a different path from that of to-day. Just as now it is necessary above all to guide men to a remembrance of their life before birth, for teachers in the ancient Mysteries it was necessary to call up in those around them a different memory.

Now a man passes his life rhythmically between two states, or really three: waking, dreaming, sleeping. Sleep takes its course in unconsciousness. The human beings of older epochs had indeed this state of unconsciousness in sleep, although it differed in certain respects from that of people to-day. They did sleep, however; they did sink down into the state of experiencing nothing in their souls, in their consciousness. But during sleep we are of course still living; we do not die and are born again when we wake. As soul and spirit we have a life during sleep, but the experience of it is completely wiped out for ordinary, everyday consciousness. People remember their waking experiences and at the most those during their dreams, but in ordinary consciousness they have no memory of anything they experience during dreamless sleep. The Mystery teachers of old treated their pupils—and through the ideas these spread abroad, all who came to them—in such a way that they were awakened to what was experienced in sleep.

Modern Initiation-knowledge has to recall what has lived in men's souls before earthly existence, whereas the old Initiation-knowledge had to evoke a memory of experiences during sleep. Thus all the knowledge that the Mystery teachers clothed in ideas was so designed that their students, or anyone else who heard it, could say: "We are being told of something we always go through in sleep. We press it down out of mind. The priests of the Mysteries have simply been enabled by their Initiation to perceive in sleep many things that are hidden from ordinary consciousness, but are all the same experienced."

Just as in the old Initiation-wisdom there was a recalling to memory of what a man had lived through in sleep, to-day there is a recalling to memory of pre-earthly life. One of the signs distinguishing the old Initiation from the new is that in the old Initiation a man was reminded of what he normally slept through, which means that he had no recollection of it in waking life. The wise men of those Mysteries drew the experiences of the night up into waking consciousness of day, and to the people they said: "During the night you dwell with your soul in the spiritual world, and the spiritual world lives in every spring, in every nightingale and every flower. Every night you enter into the midst of all that you merely perceive with your senses during the day."

And then a man could be convinced that the Gods he experienced in his waking dreams were also there outside in nature. Thus, by showing his pupil what happened in sleep, the wise teacher of the Mysteries made clear to him that divine-spiritual Beings were active out there in the realms of nature all the time. In the same way the spiritual investigator now has the task of showing that a man, before descending to Earth, was living as a spiritual being among spiritual beings in a world of spirit; and that what he experienced there he can recall on Earth in terms of concepts, of ideas.

In the Initiation-science of to-day, the real facts that distinguish sleep from waking come to be known when we advance from Imagination to Inspiration. What a man himself is as soul, as spirit, from falling asleep until he wakes, becomes clear only to Inspired knowledge, whereas the advance to Imaginative knowledge gives a man the tableau of his life. When this life-tableau unfolds for him in his waking state and with empty consciousness he is wrapped in cosmic stillness— as I have described—there enters his soul from the Cosmos, as Inspiration, the life before birth. And then his own true being appears to him in the form he lives in as a being of soul and spirit between going to sleep and waking.

Through Inspiration we become conscious of that which remains unconscious during sleep. We learn to perceive what we do as soul and spirit while asleep, and we become aware that on falling asleep the soul and spirit leave the physical body and the etheric body. The physical body is left in bed and also the etheric body—or body of formative forces, as it is seen to be in Imagination, and as I have described it. The higher members of man's nature, the astral body and the Ego-organisation, leave the physical and etheric bodies, returning to them when the time of waking comes. This cleavage of our being, which comes about in the rhythmical alternation of sleeping waking, can be seen in its real nature only through Inspiration. We then perceive that everything absorbed in ordinary waking life through our thinking, through our world of thought, is left behind. The thoughts we work upon, the thoughts we struggle with at school, whatever we have done to sharpen our earthly intelligence—all this has to be left behind with our physical body and etheric body every time we sleep. Out of these two bodies we take into the spiritual world, where as Ego and astral body we pass the time of sleeping, something quite different from anything we experience in our

waking state. When we pass from waking to sleeping we experience what is not normally brought into consciousness.
Hence, in speaking to you of these experiences, I have to
clothe them in pictorial concepts, so that they can be reflected
on with healthy human understanding. These pictorial concepts, which are mere shadows of really living thoughts, we
leave behind when we fall asleep; and we then come to live
in a world where thinking is not as it is here on Earth, but
where everything is inwardly experienced. During sleep, in
fact, we experience light unconsciously. In waking life we
think about the effects of light—how it makes shadows and
colours appear in relation to objects. All these thoughts, as I
have said, we leave behind. In sleep we enter into the weaving, living light; we pour ourselves out into the light. And as
in day time here on Earth we carry our body with us, and
also our soul and spirit, and go about on the surface of the
Earth through the air, so there, as sleeping man, we enter the
weaving, waving light, becoming ourself a being, a substance, of the living light. We become light within the light.

When a man comes to Inspired knowledge of what he
actually is each night, when this rises up into his waking
consciousness, he at once realises that during sleep he lives
like a cloud of light in cosmic light. This does not mean,
however, living simply as the substance of light, but living
in the forces which in waking life become thoughts, are
grasped as thoughts. The light then experienced is everywhere permeated by creative forces, the forces which work
inwardly in the plants, in the animals, besides existing
independently as spiritual worlds. Light is not experienced
in the same way as in the physical world but—if we may
express it figuratively—the weaving, living light is the body
of spiritual weaving, as it is also the body of each spiritual
being.

Here, as men of the physical world, we are enclosed in our
skins, and we see our fellow-men so enclosed. But in our
sleeping state we are light within the light, and other beings
are also light within the light. We do not, however, perceive
it as light in the way it is perceived in the physical world,

but—again figuratively—the clouds of light that we ourselves are, perceive other clouds of light. These clouds of
light are either another man, or some kind of being giving
new life to the plant world, or a being who, never incarnating
in a physical body, dwells always in the spiritual world.

Light, accordingly, is not experienced there as it is in
earthly life, but as living, creative spirituality. Now you know
how, as physical men here on Earth, we live in something
besides light—in the warmth our senses perceive. We feel and
experience heat and cold.

If, now, on going to sleep we pass out of our physical body
and etheric body, we live as substance of the warmth in the
cosmic substance of warmth, just as we live as light in the
light. Thus we are not only what I have called a cloud of
light, but a cloud of light permeated by weaving waves of
warmth; and what we perceive also bears warmth within it.
Just as when we are asleep, and as beings of soul and spirit,
we experience light not as light but as living spirit, and when
through Inspiration we realise ourselves and other beings also
to be living spirit—so it is in the case of warmth. It is
impossible to make any headway in the spiritual world, even
with Inspiration, if we cling to ideas acquired here on Earth.
We have already found it necessary to get used to a different
conception concerning the distance between two points, and
we must do likewise for everything else. And just as when
experiencing ourselves as light within light we actually experience ourselves as spirit in the spiritual world, so when
experiencing ourselves as warmth, within the cosmic warmth,
we do not experience this as warmth in the usual way of the
sense-world, but as weaving, strength-giving love. As the
beings of love which we are in the supersensible, we experience ourselves among beings who can do no other than draw
love out of their own essence; who can have no other existence than that of beings of love in the midst of a cosmic
existence of love. Thus do we experience ourselves, to begin
with, between going to sleep and waking, in a spiritual
existence imbued through and through with love.

Therefore, if we wish really to enter the world in which

we are every time we go to sleep until we wake, we must enhance our capacity for loving; otherwise this world is bound to remain an unknown world. Here in our earthly world it is not spiritualised love that holds sway, but a love in which the impulse of the senses prevails. In the spiritual world, however, it is spiritualised love—as I have been picturing it. Hence, whoever aspires to enter consciously the world he experiences every night has to develop his capacity for loving in the way described yesterday.

Now a man cannot find his true self without this capacity for love; for all that he really is during sleep—during a third part of his life on Earth—remains a closed book for him unless he can find his way into it through the training and enhancement of love. All that is experienced during sleep would have to remain an unsolved riddle for earthly being if they had no wish to enhance their capacity for love, so as to be able to gain some degree of knowledge about their own existence, their own being, in the changed con- dition between going to sleep and waking. But the form of activity developed in our thinking when we have our physical body and etheric body within us—that is, in our waking state—we leave behind in bed, and during sleep this becomes united in movement with the whole Cosmos. Anyone who wishes to understand clearly what goes on in the physical and etheric bodies during the night would have to be able to per- ceive from outside, while living as a being of warmth and light, how the etheric body goes on thinking all through the night.

We still have the power to think even when with our souls we are not there at all, for what we leave behind in the bed carries the waves of thinking on and on. And when we wake in the morning, we sink down into what has thus continued to think while lying there in bed. We meet our own thoughts again. They were not without life between our going to sleep and waking, although we were not present. To-morrow I shall be describing how, when thus absent, we can be much cleverer, far more intelligent, than during the day, when with our soul we are actually within our thoughts.

To-day I wished to indicate how thinking is continuous in the etheric and physical bodies, and how on waking in the morning, when we are aware of having had a dream, the dream tells us, as it were: When your soul wakes, and dives down again into the etheric body and physical body, it loses something of its power. On the one hand you have the physical body and etheric body; and on the other hand you have the astral organisation and Ego-organisation which in the morning re-enter the physical and etheric bodies. When they re-enter, it is as if a dense wave were flowing into one less dense—there is a blockage, experienced as a morning dream. The Ego and the astral body, which have been weaving all night in light and warmth, dive back into the thoughts, but by not at once understanding them, get them confused, and this blockage is experienced as a morning dream.

What more there is to say about dreams, how they are a puzzling element in human life, and the further relation between sleeping and waking—all this we will consider tomorrow.

IV

Dream Life

Between a man's waking life and his life in sleep—which yesterday I was able to picture for you at least in outline—there comes his dream life. It may have little significance for the immediate actualities of daily existence, but it has the greatest imaginable significance for a deeper knowledge of both world and man. This is not only because what a dream signifies must, in the Spiritual Science spoken of here, be fully recognised, so that the study of it may lead on to many other matters, but also because of the particular importance of dream life as a chink, shall we say, through which certain other worlds, different from the one experienced by human beings when awake, shine into this ordinary world. So it is that the puzzling elements in dream pictures often call attention both to other worlds, below or above the one normally accessible, and also give some indication of the nature of these worlds.

On the other hand it is extraordinarily difficult, from the standpoint of higher consciousness, to go deeply into the enigmas of dream life, for dreams have power to lead people into the greatest imaginable illusions. It is precisely when dreams are in question that people are inclined to go wrong over the relation of something illusory to the reality behind it. In this connection let us consider what I have said about sleep life and repeated lives on Earth.

An example of dream life, constantly recurring in one form or another, is this. We dream we have made something that, when awake, we never would have thought of making—something indeed outside the scope of anything we could have achieved in real life. We go on to dream that we cannot find this article we think we have made, and start frantically hunting for it.

Let us look at this example more closely. In the form I

have described it figures in the dream life of everyone, with
variations. But let us take a concrete instance. Let us say
that a tailor, though a tailor only in a small way, dreams that
he has made a ceremonial coat for a Minister of State. He
feels quite satisfied with his work on the coat, which should
now be lying ready. Suddenly, however, the mood of the
dream changes and when he looks all round for the coat that
has to be delivered, it is nowhere to be found.

Here you have a dream of something that could never
happen to the dreamer, but of something he can very well
imagine as highly desirable. He is only a small tailor for
lowly folk, who never could order such a coat. But occa-
sionally, in his ambitious day-dreams, he may have had the
wish to make some high-rank garment; though perhaps
incapable of it, he might still have cherished it as an ambition.

But what underlies all this? Something very real. When in
sleep a man is out of his physical and etheric bodies with
his Ego and astral body, he finds himself within the being
who goes through repeated lives on Earth. What gives inner
strength to the sleeping man, what above all is inwardly
active in his being, is the Ego together with the astral body.
These need not be limited to memories of experience in the life
just over, but can go back to other lives on Earth. I am not
theorising, but telling you of something rooted in reality,
when I say: It may be that our dreamer once had something
to do—let us say in an earlier, Roman incarnation—with
an order for a certain ceremonial toga. He need not have
been the tailor in this case; he may have been the servant, or
perhaps even the friend, of a Roman statesman. And because
at that time he had such a lively desire for his lord to appear
before the world in the most dignified possible guise, destiny
may have brought him to his present-day calling. For in
human life generally, wishes, thoughts, have an extraordinary
significance; and it is possible for the memory of what has
been lived through in a former life on Earth to play into a
man's soul and spirit, his Ego and astral body. Then, in the
morning, when he dives down with his Ego and astral body
into his etheric and physical bodies, a lingering memory of

the splendid ceremonial toga comes up against the conceptions possible for the tailor in his present life—conceptions always there in his etheric body. Then what remains of the old Roman experience is checked; it has to accommodate itself to ideas which are limited to making garments for quite lowly people. Now the soul that sinks down in this way may find it very difficult to transpose into another key the feeling it has had about the splendid toga; it is hard to relate this to a picture of the terrible clothes the tailor is obliged to make. So the picture of the toga, encountering this obstacle, changes into a picture of a present-day official uniform; and only later, when the man is well down into his etheric and physical bodies is this picture lost.

So between falling asleep and waking we have our whole human life. We have to bring to bear on it all that as earthly beings we can conceive and think, and by this means try to unravel the strange forms taken by dreams. The great difficulty is to distinguish the immediate content of the dream, which may be sheer illusion, from the reality which lies behind it, for the reality may be something quite different. But anyone who gradually gets accustomed to finding his way among all the intricacies of dream life will finally see that we need not pay much attention to the pictures conjured up before the soul, for these pictures are shaped by the etheric body left behind in bed. This etheric body is the bearer of our thoughts and conceptions and these are absent from our real being during sleep. We have to separate the content of these conceptions from what I would call the dramatic course of the dream, and learn so to fix our attention on the dramatic element that it prompts questions such as: If I had this experience in waking life, would it give me immense pleasure? And, if I felt pleasure and had a sense of relief in this dream, was I heading in the dream for a catastrophe? Was I leaving some kind of exhibition and suddenly everything got into confusion—there was a crash and a disaster? Such questions must be given first place in the study of dreams—not the thought-content but the dramatic incidents.

Someone may dream he is climbing a mountain, and the going is becoming more and more arduous. Finally, he reaches a point where he can go no further; huge obstructions tower up in front of him. He feels as though they were something important hanging over his life. That is certainly a dream a man could have; one could enlarge on it. But either he or someone else may have another dream : he is entering a cave leading to some kind of mountain cavern. After passing the entrance, there is still a certain amount of light, but it gradually becomes darker, until he arrives at a place where he is not only in complete darkness but meets with such appalling conditions, including cold, that he can penetrate no further into the cave.

Here, you see, we have two dreams quite different from one another in content. From the dramatic standpoint both deal with an undertaking that begins well, and then runs into great difficulties, ending in an insurmountable obstacle. The pictures are quite different, the dramatic course is much the same. In the supersensible world, as it were behind the scenes of life, both dreams can have the same basis. In both dreams the same thing can have affected the soul; the same thing can symbolise itself in a wide variety of picture-forms.

All this shows how we have to look for the key to a dream not—as is often done—by considering its content in an external way, but by studying its dramatic course and the effect it has on the dreamer's soul and spirit. Then, when our conceptual faculty has been strengthened by the exercises referred to in the past few days, we shall gradually progress from the illusory picture-world of the dream and be able to grasp through the dramatic element the true basis of all that we experience as supersensible reality between going to sleep and waking.

Before speaking in detail—as I shall be doing—of the dream and its relation to the physical body of man and to his spiritual element, I should like to-day to describe how, through the dream world, he is found to belong to the

Cosmos as a whole. We can see how in dreams the connection between single events in life is quite different from anything we experience when we are awake. We have just seen in the example given that in waking life things appear in a certain connection according to the laws holding good in the sense-world—a later event always follows an earlier one. The dream takes events that could happen in the sense-world and makes them chaotic. Everything becomes different; everything is broken up. All that is normally bound to the Earth by gravity, like man himself, is suddenly—in a dream—able to fly. A man will perform skilful flying feats without an aeroplane. And a mathematical problem, for instance, such as we may strain every nerve to solve in ordinary life, appears in a dream to be mere child's play. The solution is probably forgotten on waking—well, that is a personal misfortune—but at any rate one gets the idea that the obstacles which hamper our thinking in daily life have disappeared. In effect, everything in daily life with definite connections loses them to a certain extent in dreams. If we want to picture what actually happens—or appears to happen—in a dream, we can imagine the following. Into a glass of water we put some kind of soluble salt in crystalline form, and watch it dissolve. We see how its clear-cut forms melt away, how they take on fantastic shapes, until all the salt is dissolved, and we are left with a glass of more or less homogenous fluid.

This is very like the kind of experience we have inwardly in dreams. The dream we have as we go to sleep and the dream we have just before waking both draw on the experiences of the day, break them up and give them all sorts of fantastic forms—at least we call them fantastic from the point of view of ordinary consciousness. The dissolving of a salt in a liquid is a good simile for the kind of thing that happens inwardly in a dream.

It will not be easy for those who have grown up in the world of present-day ideas to grasp without prejudice facts of this kind; for people to-day—especially those who regard themselves as scientific—know remarkably little about certain things. In truth I am not saying this because I like picking holes in science. That is not at all my intention. I value the scientific approach and should certainly never wish to see it replaced by the work of amateurs or dilettantti. Even from the standpoint of Spiritual Science the great progress, the strict truthfulness and trustworthiness, of science to-day, must be given full recognition. That is an understood thing. Nevertheless, the following has to be said.

When people to-day wish to know something, they turn to earthly objects and processes. They observe these and from their observations they work out laws of nature. They also make experiments to bring to light the secrets of nature, and the results of their experiments are further laws. Thus they come to laws of a certain type, and this they call science. Then they turn their gaze to the vastness of the heavens; they see—let us say—the wonderful spiral nebulae, where they see individual cosmic bodies emerging, and so on. To-day we photograph such things and see much more detail than telescopic observation can give. Now how do astronomers proceed to learn what is going on in those far celestial spaces? They turn to the laws of nature, laws founded on earthly conditions and earthly experiments, and then start speculating as to how, in conformity with those laws, a spiral nebula could have taken form in distant space. They form hypotheses and theories about the arising and passing away of worlds by treating facts discovered in their laboratories about manganese, oxygen, hydrogen, as laws that still hold good in heavenly spheres. When by such means a new substance is discovered, unconscious indications are sometimes given that science here is not on firm ground. Hydrogen has been found everywhere in the vastness of space, and helium, for example; and another substance that has been given a curious name, curious because it points to the confused thinking that comes in. It has been called nebulium. Thinking itself becomes nebulous here, for we find nebulium in company with helium and hydrogen. When people are so simple that they apply as laws of nature knowledge acquired in earthly laboratories, and indulge in speculation about what goes on outside in the wide realms of space, after the manner of the Swedish thinker

Arrhenius*—who has done untold harm in this connection—
they are bound to fall from one error into another, if they are
unable to consider without prejudice the following.

Again I should like to start with a comparison. From the
history of science you will know that Newton, the English
physicist and natural philosopher, established the theory of
what is called gravitation—the effect of weight in universal
space. He extended this law, illustrated in the ordinary falling
of a stone attracted by the Earth, to the reciprocal relation
between all bodies in the Cosmos. He stated also that the
strength of gravity diminishes with distance. For any physi-
cists who may be present I will remind you of the law—
gravity decreases with the square of the distance. Thus if the
distance doubles, gravity becomes four times weaker, and so
on.

For such a force it is quite right to set up a law of this
kind. But while we are bound to purely physical existence,
it is impossible to think out this law far enough for universal
application. Just imagine in the case of a cosmic body how
the force of gravity must diminish with distance. It is strong
at first and then grows weaker, still weaker, always weaker
and weaker.

It is the same with the spreading out of light. As it spreads
out from a given source, it becomes always weaker and weaker.
This is recognised by scientists today. But they fail to recognise something else—that when they establish laws of nature
in a laboratory, and then clothe them in ideas, the truth and
content of these laws diminish as distance from the earth
increases. When, therefore, a law is established on Earth for
the combining of elements—oxygen, hydrogen or any others
—and if a law of gravity is set up for the earth, then, as

* Svante August Arrhenius, a pioneer of modern physical
chemistry; gained Nobel prize for his work on electrical conduc-
tion in dilute solutions. In one of his books, *Das Werden der
Welten*, 1907 (English translation, Worlds in the Making, 1908),
he suggested the name "nebulium" for a hypothetical gas represented by certain then unidentified lines in the spectra of gaseous
nebulae. In 1927 it was shown that the lines are due to singly
and doubly ionised atoms of oxygen.

one goes out into cosmic space, the efficacy of this law will also decrease. If here in my laboratory I set up a law of nature and then apply it to a spiral nebula in far-off cosmic space, I am doing just the same as if I were to light a candle and then believe that if I could project its rays through cosmic space on to the spiral nebula, the candle would give the same amount of light out there. I am making precisely the same mistake if I believe that a finding I establish in my laboratory is valid in the far reaches of the Cosmos. So arises the widely prevalent mistaken idea that what is discovered quite rightly to be a natural law in a laboratory down here on earth can be applied also throughout the vast spaces of the heavens.

Now man himself is not exempt from the laws we encounter when earthly laws, such as those of gravity or of light, no longer hold good. If anyone wished to discover a set of laws other than our laws of nature, he would have to journey further and further away from the Earth; and to find such laws in a more intimate, human way, he goes to sleep. When awake, we are in the sphere where the laws of nature hold sway and in all that we do we are subject to them. For example, we decide to lift a hand or arm, and the chemico-physical processes taking place in the muscles, the mechanical play of the bony structure, are governed by the laws discovered in earthly laboratories, or by other means of observation. But our soul goes out in sleep from our physical and etheric bodies, and enters a world not subject to the laws of nature. That is why dreams are a mockery of those laws. We enter an entirely different world—a world to which we grow accustomed in sleep, just as when, awake in our physical body, we accustom ourselves to the world of the senses. This different world is not governed by our laws of nature; it has laws of its own. We dive into this world every night on going out of our physical and etheric bodies. Dreams are a power which forcibly opposes nature's laws.

While I am dreaming, the dream itself shows me that I am living in a world opposed to these laws, a world which refuses to be subject to them. While going to sleep in the evening and moving out of my physical and etheric bodies, I am still living half under the laws of nature, although I am already entering the world where they cease to be valid. Hence arises the confusion in the dream between natural laws and super-sensible laws; and it is the same while we are waking up again.

Thus we can say that each time we go to sleep we sink into a world where the laws of nature are not valid; and each time we wake we leave that world to re-enter a world subject to those laws. If we are to imagine the actual process, it is like this. Picture the dream-world as a sea in which you are living, and assume that in the morning you wake out of the waves of dream-life—it is as if you arose out of the surge of those waves. You move from the realm of supersensible law into the realm of intellectual, material law. And it seems to you as though everything you see in sharp outlines on waking were born out of the fluid and the volatile. Suppose you are looking, say, at a window. If you first dream of the window, it will indeed appear as though born out of something flowing, something indefinite perhaps, imbued with all manner of fiery flames. So the window rises up, and if you had been dreaming vividly you would realise how the whole sharply outlined world of our ordinary consciousness is born out of this amorphous background—as if out of the sea arose waves which then took on the forms of the everyday world.

Here we come to a point where—if as present-day men we are investigating these things anew—we feel reverent wonder at the dreamlike imaginations of earlier humanity. As I have said during these days, if we look back to the imaginations experienced even in waking life by the souls of those early peoples, imaginations embodied in their myths, legends and sayings of the gods, which all passed before them in so hazy a way compared with our clear perception of nature— when we look back on all this with the help of what can now be discovered quite independently of those old dreamy imaginations, we are filled with veneration and wonder. And if in this sphere we search again for truth, it echoes down from ancient Greece in a word which shows that the Greeks still retained some knowledge of these things. They said to themselves: "Something underlies the shaping of the world, something out of which all definite forms arise, but it is accessible only when we leave behind the world of the senses while we are asleep and dreaming." The Greeks called this something, "Chaos". All speculation, all abstract inquiry into the nature of this chaos, has been fruitless, but men to-day come near to it when it plays into their dreams. Yet in mediaeval times there was still some knowledge of a super-sensible, scarcely material substance lying behind all material substance, for a so-called quintessence, a fifth mode of being, was spoken of together with the four elements: earth, water, air, fire—and quintessence.

Or we find something that recalls the mediaeval vision when the poet with his intuitive perception says that the world is woven out of dreams. The Greeks would have said: The world is woven out of the chaos you experience when you leave the sense-world and are free of the body. Hence, to understand what the Greeks meant by "chaos" we must turn not to the material but to the supersensible world.

When from the point of view of what is revealed to us on the path I have been describing here—the path leading through Imagination, Inspiration, Intuition, to higher knowledge and supersensible worlds—when we follow all that goes on during our dreaming, sleeping and re-awaking, then we see that a man sleeps himself out of his daytime state into his life of sleep, out of which dreams may arise in a way that is chaotically vague, but also inwardly consistent. Behind, in bed, the physical body is left with the etheric body which is interwoven with the physical, giving it life, form, and power of growth. This twofold entity is left in the bed.

But another twofold entity goes out during sleep into a form of supersensible existence which I might also describe to you in relation still to dream existence. For the higher knowledge given by Imagination, Inspiration, Intuition, it presents itself in the following way.

When a man goes out from his physical body and etheric body, his individuality resides in his astral body. As I said before, there is no need to be held up by words. We must have words, but we could just as well call the astral body something else. I am about to describe something concerning the astral body, and we shall see that the name is not important but rather the concepts that can be attached to it. Now, this astral body is made up of processes. Something happens in a man which develops out of his physical and etheric bodies, and it is these happenings which represent the astral body; whereas our concepts, our thoughts, are left behind in the etheric body.

Within the astral body there is spiritualised light, and cosmic warmth permeated by the force of the capacity for love. All this is present in the astral body, and at the time of waking it dives down into the etheric body. There it is held up and appears as the weaving, the action, of the dream. It may also appear in this way when, freeing itself from the physical and etheric bodies, it leaves the world of concepts. Thus it belongs to the nature of the astral body to carry us out from our physical and etheric bodies.

As I have already said, the astral body is that part of our being which actually opposes the laws of nature. From morning to night, from waking till going to sleep, we are subject to these laws—laws which in relation to space and time we can grasp through mathematics. When we sleep, however, we extricate ourselves both from the laws of nature and from the laws of mathematics—from the latter laws because our astral body has nothing to do with the abstractions of three-dimensional space. It has its own mathematics, following a straight line in one dimension only. I shall have to speak again about this question of dimensions. It is truly the astral body that releases us from the laws of nature, by which we are fettered between waking and sleeping; it is also the astral body that bears us into a completely different world, the supersensible world.

To describe this process schematically we must say : When we are awake we carry on our life in the sphere where the laws of nature hold good; but on going to sleep we go out from there with our astral body. While we are living here in our physical and etheric bodies, our astral body, as a member of our being, is subject to the laws of nature, and in all its movements and functions lives entirely under those laws. On leaving the physical and etheric bodies, the astral body enters the supersensible world and is subject to supersensible laws, which are completely different. The astral body, too, is changed. While we are awake it is, as it were, in the strait-jacket of nature's laws. Then it goes to sleep, which means that it leaves the physical and etheric bodies and moves in a world whose laws are in tune with its own freedom. Now what is this world? It is a world giving freedom of movement to the Ego-organisation which, together with the astral body, is then outside the physical and etheric bodies. Every night the Ego becomes free in the world to which the astral body carries it—free to carry out its own will in this world where the laws of nature no longer prevail.

In the time between going to sleep and waking, when our astral body is no longer subject to these laws, and we are in a world where the force of gravity, the law of energy, in fact all laws of that kind have ceased to be valid, the way is clear for those moral impulses which down here, during waking life, can find expression only under the constraint of the world of the senses and its ordering. Between sleeping and waking the Ego lives in a world where the moral law has the same force and power as the laws of nature have down here. And in that world where in sleep it is set free from laws of nature, the Ego can prepare itself for what it will have to be doing after death. In coming lectures we shall be speaking about this road from death to a new birth.

Between going to sleep and waking, the Ego can prepare in picture form, in Imaginations—which are not concepts, but strong impulses—for what it will have to strive for in the later reality of the spirit. When the Ego has gone through the gate of death, moral laws take the place that the laws of nature hold in the physical world of the senses.

Thus we can say that the Ego, even as a quite small spiritual seed, works upon what it has to carry through after death in the world of the spirit. Here, in what the Ego works upon in picture form during sleep, are indications of what we shall be able to carry over—not through any laws of nature but by reason of the spiritual world—from this life on Earth to the next. The causal effects of the moral impulses we have absorbed can be followed up here only when we have disposed ourselves in inward obedience to them. Just as the Ego during sleep works upon the moral impulses, and continues its work between death and a new birth, so these impulses acquire the force that otherwise the laws of nature possess, and in the next human body, which we shall bear in our following life on earth, they clothe themselves in our moral disposition, in our temperament, in the whole trend of our character—all wrongly ascribed to heredity. This has to be worked upon during sleep by the Ego when, freed by the astral body from the world of nature, it enters a purely spiritual world. Thus we see how in sleep a man prepares and grows familiar with his own future.

What, then, do the dreams show us? I would put it like this. During sleep too the Ego is active, but what it does is shown us by dreams in illusory pictures. In earthly life we are unable to take in what is already being woven during sleep for our next life on Earth. At the beginning of this lecture I explained how the dream, in the same confused way in which it presents the experiences of a past incarnation, also shows, in a chaotic form, what is prepared as a seed for humanity in future times.

Hence the right interpretation of dreams leads us to recognise that they are like a window through which we have only to look in the right way—a window into the supersensible world. Behind this window the Ego is actively weaving, and this weaving goes on from one earthly life to the next. When we can interpret a dream rightly, then, through this window from the transitory world in which we live as earthly men, we already perceive that everlasting world, that eternity, to which in our true inner being we belong.

V

The Relation of Man
to the Three Worlds

Dreams, of which I have already said something, pointing out that they should not be given too much importance in ordinary life on earth, are nevertheless of immeasurable significance to those wishing to gain knowledge of man's relation to the supersensible world. They do indeed lead to that realm of experience where a man comes in contact with the supersensible world, and the laws of nature cease to hold good. Thus the world of dream-pictures is really like a veil concealing the spiritual world, and we can say: Here we have a man, and there a dream-veil behind which lies the spiritual world. It makes a great difference, however, whether we enter the spiritual world unconsciously, as we do in dreams, or consciously through Imagination and Inspiration. For if we enter it consciously, everything there appears different from the physical world of nature. Behind the veil of the dream, behind what the Greeks called "chaos", the moral world is found to be just as real as is the world of nature here in the sense-world, where the laws of nature rule. But the chaotic quality of the dream, its whirling confusion, show that its connection with the world lying behind the veil of chaos is a very special one.

It is really possible to speak of this world only when one's studies have reached the point to which these lectures have brought us. All that in his ordinary state of consciousness a man sees of the external world is merely its outward manifestation; in reality this is a great illusion. For behind it all is that spiritual reality which is active in it. When a man dreams, he actually sinks down into this spiritual reality, though without being properly prepared, so that what he meets appears to him in this whirling confusion. Thus, to begin with, our chief task is to learn why in dreams a man enters a world which, compared with that of nature, is so disorganised, so chaotic.

To help us on, therefore, in our study of dreams, I must now tell you something of what Imagination and Inspiration can perceive in the spiritual world.

We find above all that when through Imagination and Inspiration we enter the spiritual world in full consciousness, it immediately appears to us to be threefold. Hence we can speak of the world, and of our theme, the evolution of the world and of man, only when we have come to the point we have now reached. Only now can I speak of how a man, confronted by the external world, by all that manifests itself to the senses, is really facing the spiritual world in its threefold nature—facing actually three worlds. Once the veil has been lifted which creates the chaos, we no longer have one world only before us, but three worlds, and each of the three has its definite connection with the human being.

When we succeed in penetrating this veil of chaos—later I shall be showing how we can also describe this as crossing the threshold of the spiritual world—we perceive the three worlds. The first of the three is really the world we have just left, somewhat transformed but still there for spiritual existence. When the veil of chaos has been thrust aside, this world appears as though it were a memory. We have passed over into the spiritual world; and just as here we remember certain things, so in the spiritual world we remember what constitutes the physical world of the senses. Here, then, is the first of the three worlds.

The second world we encounter is the one I have called in my book, *Theosophy,* the soul-world.

And the third world, the highest of the three, is the true spiritual world, the world of the spirit.

To begin with, I shall give you only a schematic account of all this, but from the way these three worlds are related to man you will gather many things about them. To these three worlds as they appear in three ascending stages—the lowest, the middle one, and the highest—I will then relate man's three members—the head; then the breast-organisation embracing all that is rhythmical, the breathing system and blood circulation; thirdly, the metabolic-limb system, which includes nutrition, digestion and the distribution throughout the body of the products of digestion, all of which engender movement. All this has to do with the metabolic-limb system. If this scheme were drawn, there would have to be a closed circle for the breast; for the head a circle left open, and open also for the limb system. When perceived physically, man's head appears to be closed above and would have to be drawn so, but perceived spiritually, it is open. The part of a man which does not belong at all to the realm of the spirit is the bony system, which is entirely of a physical nature; and when spiritually you study the human head, its thick skull is not seen. Only the skin is visible where the hair grows.

When this is looked at spiritually, however, something else appears. Ordinary hair is not there at all, but purely spiritual hair; in other words, rays which penetrate into the human organism and are held back, to some extent, only by the physical hair. But it is just where there is bone in the organism that the spirit can enter most easily, and this it does in the form of rays. So, on first looking at a man with your physical eyes. you see his physical form with the head above, and on his head—if he is not already bald—there is hair. But then, where the dome of the skull comes, spiritually you see nothing of the physical man; you see rays, sun-like rays, pouring into him from the spiritual worlds.

Thus the reason for the circle not being closed for the head is that the surrounding bony vault of the skull enables the spirit to have continual access there.

Nothing in a man is without purpose. By deliberate intent of the ruling powers—one might say—he has been given a head thus closed above, for here the spirit has the easiest access to his inner being because of the very thickness of the bone.

When we are in a position to observe man spiritually, we are astonished to discover how empty his head is of anything drawn from his own inner being. As regards the spiritual, he has almost nothing in him to fill the hollow globe sitting on

his shoulders. Everything spiritual has to enter it from outside.

It is not thus with the other members of the human organism; as we shall soon hear, these are by their very nature
spiritual. We can distinguish in man three members—head, or
nerves and senses system, rhythmic system, metabolic-limb
system, and they have a quite definite relation to the three
worlds : the physical world, the soul-world, and the spiritual
world. I will now go further into this.

First of all, it will be well to distinguish, in each of the
three worlds, *substance* from *activity*. In reality, substance
and activity are one, but they work in different ways in the
world. You gain a clear idea of this from the substance of
your own being. You have substance in your arm, and when
this substance is out of order you will feel pain of some
kind; it is obvious that something within the substance of the
arm has gone wrong. If the activity of the arm is not properly
controlled, you may perhaps hit your neighbour and *he* feels
pain. This shows that the activity is out of gear. Nevertheless,
though manifesting outwardly in different ways, the substance and activity in your arm are one.

If now we turn to the human head, we find its substance
derived entirely from the physical world. During the formation
of the human embryo the substance of the head comes from
the parents; and the subsequent development of the head, and
of the whole head and nerve-senses system, depends for its
substance entirely on the earthly-material world. On the
other hand, all the activity that has to do with the plastic
forming of a man's head, the activity by means of which its
substance is given *shape,* comes entirely from the spiritual
world. So that in respect of activity, the head is entirely a
spiritual formation. Therefore the head has to be left open—
in a spiritual sense—so that activity can play into it.

At any time of life you can thus say : The substance of
my head comes entirely from the Earth, but it is put together and plastically formed in such a way that it cannot be

the work of earthly forces. The forms of this human head are shaped entirely from the spiritual world; they might be called a heavenly creation. Anyone who contemplates spiritually the human head, in relation to the world, has to go far and deep.

Now in the same way he turns his gaze to a plant. He says to himself : The plant has a definite form. Its substance is drawn from the earth, but its form comes from the etheric world—hence still from the spatial world.

Then he looks at an animal. The animal—he will say to himself—derives the substance of its head entirely from the world of space, but something spiritual certainly flows into its activity.

When we come to the human head, however, we find for the first time that something of the highest spirituality, something that can be called heavenly, is playing in. We see that the human head could never arise from earthly forces, though its substance is taken from earthly materials. So in the human head, which is itself a kind of miniature Cosmos, the spiritual world builds up a form out of earthly substance.

It is precisely the reverse with the metabolic-limb system, which embraces the organs for external movement—legs, arms—and the extension of these within the body—the digestive system.

For the present I am leaving out the middle system—the rhythmical system which embraces breathing and the circulation of the blood. I will deal now with the system which brings together the processes of digestion and nourishment, and the inner combustion which enables a man to move.

Now the substance of this metabolic-limb system is not derived from the Earth. Improbable as it may sound, you bear within your metabolic-limb man something which is not of earthly origin but consists wholly of substance from the third world, the world of the spirit. You may say : But I can see my legs; they are physically perceptible, which they would not be if they consisted of spiritual substance. This objection is quite justified, but there is something more to be considered.

Your real legs are indeed spiritual throughout; your real

arms too; but the material for them is provided by your head. The head is the organ which fills spirit arms, spirit hands, spirit legs, spirit feet, with substance; and this substance penetrates into the spirituality of the limbs and of the digestive organs. So that something which in reality belongs entirely to the spiritual world is permeated, flooded, with physical matter by the head. That is why it is so difficult to grasp with the ideas of physical science that a man consists of head-breast-limbs-digestive organs. People think of the head as being there at the top, and they assume that when a man is decapitated he has no head left. It is not so, however; a man is substantially head all over. Even right to the end of his big toe he is head, for his head sends down its substance there. It is only the substance of the head that is earthly in origin, and the head gives its earthly-material character to the other substances; while the substance of the metabolic-limb organs comes from the spiritual world.

If through vigorous auto-suggestion of a negative kind we can suggest away the head of a man, so that in appearance he is headless, and if we can do this not only in thought but so that we really see the man as headless, then the rest of his organism also disappears; with the head goes the whole of the man as a being perceptible to the senses. And if the head is then to be there for us at all, the rest of the man has to be perceived spiritually. For in reality we go about under the imprint of higher worlds, with spirit legs, spirit arms, and it is only the head that fills them with physical matter.

On the other hand the forces, the activity, for all that makes up the metabolic-limb man are drawn from the physical world. If you make a step forward or lift an arm, the mechanism involved, and even the chemical processes that take place in moving an arm or leg, or the chemical processes in the digestive organs—all this activity is earthly. So that in your limbs you bear invisible substance, but forces drawn from earthly life. Hence we are built up as regards our head and its substance out of the Earth, but this same head is permeated with heavenly forces. In our limbs we are built up entirely from heavenly substance; but the forces playing into this heavenly substance during our life on Earth are earthly forces—gravitation and other physical and chemical forces all belonging to the Earth.

You see, therefore, that head and limbs are opposites. The head consists of earthly matter and is given plastic form by heavenly activity. The limbs and the digestive system are formed wholly of heavenly substance, and would not be visible were they not saturated with earthly substance by the head. But when anyone walks, or grasps something, or digests food, the heavenly substance makes use of earthly forces in order that life on Earth, from birth to death, may be carried on.

In this complicated way does a man stand in relation to the three worlds. The spiritual world participates with its activity in the head; with its substance it participates in a man's third organisation, his metabolic-limb system. The lowest world, the world most dominated by the senses, participates through its activity in the metabolism and the movement of the limbs, and through its substance in the head; whereas the substance in a man's third system is wholly spiritual.

In the middle system, which embraces the breathing and the circulation of the blood, spiritual activity and material substance work into each other. The spiritual activity, flowing through the movement of our breathing and the beating of our heart, is always accompanied to some extent by substantiality. And, in the same way, the substantiality of earthly existence, inasmuch as oxygen streams into the breathing, is to some extent accompanied by earthly activity. So you see that in the middle man, in man's second system, everything flows together—heavenly substance and activity flow in here; earthly activity and substance flow in there. By this means we are made receptive both to the activity of the middle world and to its substantiality.

So in this middle man there is a great deal of intermingling and for this reason we need our wonderfully perfect rhythmical system—the rhythm of the heart, the rhythm of the lungs in breathing. All the intermingling of activity and substance is balanced, harmonised, melodised, through these rhythms, and this can happen because man is organised for it.

In the head system and the limb system, activity and substantiality come from quite different sources, but in the middle system they come from all three worlds and in a variety of ways—at one place activity accompanied by substance, in another place substance accompanied by activity; here pure activity, there pure substance—all these variations flow through the middle man. If as a doctor you take a man's pulse, you can really feel there the balancing of the heavenly nature of the soul against earthly activity and substantiality. Again, if you observe the breathing, you can feel a man's inner striving for balance between the various agencies which relate him to the middle world.

All this is very complicated, you will say. It is true that a lecture-course is generally easy to understand up to a certain stage, but when it comes to the point where man's relation to the world has to be grasped, people often say : "This is becoming very difficult—we can't keep up with it."

But look—with really flexible thinking, free from prejudice, you will be able to keep up. And for anyone who thinks in this way, with healthy human understanding, there is a certain consolation. As I said before, the actual thrusting aside of the veil of chaos and the entry into the threefold world, which sends its activity and substance into the physical world in so vastly complicated a way—this experience is so bewildering that full warning of it is given before the threshold is crossed. I will put it pictorially, but in full accord with the facts. The warning is : "If you are not willing to forgo what you have regarded as ordinary naturalistic logic and as the customary connections between things, if you are reluctant to leave behind this physical cloak, it is better that you should not enter the spiritual world, for there you will be obliged to make use of other associations of ideas, other orderings, and a completely different logic. If you want to take anything of your physical logic with you into the spiritual world, you will quite certainly get confused." And among the matters that have to do with preparing ourselves for meditation and concentration, we have to remember the warning never to carry over the logic of the sense-world into the logic of the spiritual world.

This is the important warning given by that power we may call the Guardian of the Threshold—of whom we shall hear more in later lectures—to those who wish to pierce behind the veil.

But when we wish to return to the physical world, we receive from the Guardian another warning, clear and forcible. So long as we are men of Earth we return, or we should never get away from happenings in the spiritual world, and our deserted physical body would die. We must always return. In accordance with naturalistic logic we have to eat, drink, and adapt ourselves every day to customary activities. We are obliged to re-enter the world where things follow a naturalistic course—where, for example, we are called to meals at the usual hours. So, when we are returning from the spiritual world to the physical world, we must—to avoid an impossible situation—pay heed to the second warning given by the Guardian who stands where the veil of chaos separates the physical sense-world from the spiritual world. This, then, is the warning: "During your life on Earth, never for a moment forget that you have been in the spiritual world; then and only then, during the times you have to spend in the physical world, will you be able to guide your steps with certainty."

Thus at the threshold of this threefold spiritual world, to which a man is related through his three members in the way described, he is warned to lay aside all naturalistic logic, to leave behind this cloak of the senses and to go forward prepared to adapt himself to a spiritual logic, spiritual thinking and the spiritual association of ideas. On his return he is given a second warning, just as stern, even sterner than the first: never for a moment to forget his experience in the spiritual world—in other words, not to confine himself in ordinary consciousness merely to the impulses of the sense-world, and so on, but always to be conscious that to his physical world he has to be a bearer of the spiritual.

You will see that the two warnings differ considerably from one another. At the entrance to the spiritual world the Guardian of the Threshold says: Forget the physical world of the senses while here you are acquiring knowledge of the spiritual. But on your return to the physical world the Guardian's warning is: Never forget, even in the physical world on Earth, your experiences in the heavenly world of the spirit; keep your memory of them alive.

With reference to what I said last time, there is another considerable difference between the men of an older evolutionary epoch and those of the present time. In the case of those I pictured coming to the Mystery centres as inspired pupils, or just as ordinary folk, the transition from sleeping to waking and from waking to sleeping was not made without their being instinctively aware of the Guardian of the Threshold. Three or four thousand years ago, as men were entering sleep, there arose in their souls like a dream a picture of the Guardian. They passed him by. And as they were returning from sleep to ordinary life, once again this picture appeared. The warnings they received on entering and leaving the spiritual world were not so clear as the warnings which I have said are given to those entering the spiritual world through Inspiration and Imagination. But as they fell asleep, and again as they awoke, they had a dreamlike experience of passing the Guardian of the Threshold, not unlike their other instinctive perceptions of the spiritual world. Further progress in the evolution of humanity—as we shall see in later lectures —required that man should gain his freedom by losing his spiritual vision, and he had to forfeit that half-sleeping, half-waking state during which he was able to behold, at least in a kind of dream, the majestic figure of the Guardian of the Threshold.

Nowadays, between going to sleep and waking, a man passes the Guardian but does not know it. He is blind and deaf to the Guardian, and that is why he finds himself in a dreamworld which is so completely disorganised.

Now consider quite impartially the different way in which the people of older epochs knew how to speak of their dreams. Because of ignoring the Guardian every morning, every evening, and twice every time he takes an afternoon nap, a man to-day experiences this utter disorder and chaos in his dream-world. This can be seen in the form taken by any dream.

Only think : when we cross the Threshold—and we do so each time we go to sleep—there stands the majestic Guardian. He cannot be ignored without everything we meet in the spiritual world becoming disordered. How this happens is best seen in the metamorphosis undergone by the orderly thinking proper to the physical, naturalistic world when this passes into the imagery of dreams. Individual dreams can show this very clearly.

In the physical, naturalistic world people behave as they learn to do in accordance with its conditions. We will take a case in point. Someone goes for a walk. Now in a town to-day, you will agree, certain walks are taken particularly for the experiences they offer. For example, during a walk people meet friends; they can show off their clothes if so inclined, both to those they know and to strangers. All this can be experienced during a walk and the point of it is that it gives occasion for us to have thoughts, ideas, so that we are able—only our head-organisation is here concerned—to say : "I think." By virtue of this "I think" it is possible to experience in the outside world the kind of thing I have just been describing. One meets other people, and it is an experience for them too. One displays one's clothes, perhaps a pretty face into the bargain. What matters is the experience. In this seeing other people, however, in this exhibiting to them our outward appearance, feeling also plays its part. One thing pleases us, another does not. Sympathies and antipathies are aroused. We like it when the people we meet say what is agreeable to us, and we don't like it when they say the opposite. Hence what is experienced on such walks is closely connected with what the head conceives by means of this "I think." It is connected through the "I feel" of the rhythmical man—that is, with feelings of sympathy and antipathy. Because with this second member of our being we can say "I feel", we are able to enlarge the experiences that come to us in thought during a walk.

But the third member of man also plays a part on this walk,

if we are fully awake. Here we must turn to certain intimate details of human experience. There is a general feeling that civilised people to-day do not show themselves in public without clothes, do not go for walks without them; there is a general antipathy towards nudity and sympathy towards being properly clad. This goes right into our impulses of will. We clothe ourselves—even doing so in a specified way. Here the will comes into its own, the third member of the human organisation. Clothing ourselves is thus connected with the part of us that enables us to say "I will".

I think   I feel

I will

So, through being able to say "I will," we go for our walks clothed. When we are awake in the physical world, all this is regulated by the logic of this world. Either we are brought up to it, or we learn to conform to the outer conditions prescribed by the physical world and its logic. If we do not conform, but go for a walk without our clothes, then something within us is out of order. The ordering of the physical world, the logic of the physical world, go together in all this. It never occurs to us on a walk to wish to meet people without clothes. Here, our soul-experience is determined by the ordering of the world. And this shows how the three—I think, I feel, I will—are all connected with one another. It is the world that does this; the external world leads us to form this connection between thinking, feeling and willing.

When, ignoring the Guardian, we cross the Threshold, we confront three worlds, and we can make nothing of them because we partly carry over into the world of spirit the outlook we are familiar with in the waking world. The spiritual world, however, asserts its own order to a certain exent. Then the following may come about. Imagine you are asleep in bed. At first with your feeling, with the middle part of your being, you are entirely under the influence of sleep. Then the coverlet slips; part of your body gets chilled, and it enters your dream consciousness that some part of you is unclothed.

Now, because you are all at sea in the spiritual world and do not connect the sensation with any particular part of yourself, this feeling spreads, and you fancy you are without any clothes at all. It may be only a bit of your body that is exposed, but that bit becoming cold makes you feel bare all over.

Now in your dream you are still concerned with an impulse of will holding good when you are awake—which is to put on clothes when bare. In your sleep, however, you feel: I cannot put them on, something is preventing me. You are unable to move your limbs and you become conscious of this in your dream.

You see how it is. These two things, I feel I've nothing on, and I cannot put on my clothes—the physical world being no longer there to combine the two, one of which belongs to world II, the other to world I—are wrongly combined in your dream. And because in that same night you had thought about going for a walk, this also enters the course of the dream. Three separate conditions arise: I am going for a walk; I am horrified to find I have nothing on; I cannot put my clothes on.

Now just think. These three things, which in our ordinary materialistic life can be logically combined, fall asunder when, in passing by, you ignore the Guardian of the Threshold.

In world I: the walk

In world II: being without clothes

In world III: the experience of not being able to put on clothes. In this situation you feel yourself in three parts, among strangers, exposed to view on all sides without clothes and without power to put them on. That is your dream experience. What is connected for you in ordinary life through natural logic is separated in your dream and connected, chaotically, in conformity with the custom you take with you across the Threshold. You connect it as if in the spiritual world, too, one has to concern oneself with garments. Because of ignoring the Guardian of the Threshold, you carry over into the spiritual world a custom suited to the physical world. You connect the three worlds chaotically, according to the laws of the physical world, and you feel yourself to be in this situation.

In countless dreams the essential thing is that when we pass the Threshold without heeding the Guardian's warning, what we perceive here in the physical, naturalistic world as a harmonious unity falls apart, and we are confronted by three different worlds. By faithfully observing the warning given by the Guardian of the Threshold, we must find the way to unite these three worlds. To-day, a man in his dreams finds himself faced by these three worlds—it was not so to the same extent for anyone in older epochs, as can be seen from the dreams recorded in the Old Testament—and he then tries to connect the three worlds in accordance with laws valid in physical life. That is the reason for the chaotic connections in the three worlds, as they are experienced by a man of to-day.

You will see, therefore, that dreams can show us this serious fact—that when we cross the Threshold to the spiritual world we are at once faced with three worlds, and that we have both to enter them and to leave them in the right way. Dreams can teach us a very great deal about the physical world of the senses, as it is to-day, and also about that other world—the world of soul and spirit.

VI

The Ruling of Spirit in Nature

Yesterday I tried to show how the confusion in dreams arises from the fact that during sleep a man crosses the so-called Threshold unconsciously or half-consciously. Leaving the physical world of the senses, he enters the spiritual world and there encounters three worlds—a memory of the ordinary physical world, the soul world, and the real world of spirit. Events both inward and outward, experienced in our ordinary earthly life, are gathered together from what these three worlds reveal. But they are split apart when in sleep we enter the supersensible world, and what we experience is not then related to the world where it belongs. That is why, for the usual memory-consciousness, deceptions and illusions arise in dreams. Imaginative consciousness does not see the dream merely in this way, but makes it an object of observation, just as we look towards a distant point in physical space—though now, with Imagination, we look towards something distant in time. We do not simply remember what is dreamt; we look at it, and so for the first time we arrive at a true conception of what a dream is. Thus we find how a dream is interpreted rightly only when we do not relate it to the physical, naturalistic world, but to the spiritual—above all, in most cases, to the moral world. The dream will never tell what it is expressing if its content is given a physical interpretation, but only when the interpretation is in accordance with the spiritually moral.

To illustrate this, let us turn to the confusion of the dream I told you about yesterday—the dream in which someone going for a walk is suddenly overcome with shame at finding himself without clothes in a crowded street. I remarked how the whole mood of soul in dream-consciousness is due to our confronting three different worlds. Looking at a dream of this kind in the right way, however, we see that although its content appears to belong to the realm of the senses, yet through this medium the spiritual-moral is seeking to reveal itself. Hence, anyone having such a dream ought not to look at the immediate, symbolical course it takes, but should ask himself : Haven't I sometimes had a tendency in daytime consciousness not to be completely truthful about myself with others? Haven't I perhaps been too fond of following the fashion in what I wear—altogether too apt to take refuge in convention? Is it not a characteristic of mine to give people a false impression of what I really am?

When anyone lets his thoughts take this course, he gradually arrives at the moral, spiritual interpretation of the dream. He says to himself : When during sleep I was in the supersensible world, I met with spiritual beings there—they told me that I should not be present in a cloak of falsehood, but as I really am inwardly, in soul and spirit.

When we interpret dreams in this way, we come to their moral, spiritual truth. A whole host of dreams can be interpreted thus.

People of an older chapter in history, who even in the dreamy symbolism of sleep were conscious of the Guardian of the Threshold, took to heart his warning not to carry with them what belongs to the physical world of the senses when they enter the spiritual world. Had these men dreamt they had no clothes on in the street, it would never have occurred to them that they ought to have been ashamed; this is something that holds good for the physical world, for a man's physical body. They would have given heed to the warning that what holds good for the physical does not hold good in the spiritual world, and that what appears in the spiritual world is being said to human beings by the Gods. A dream, therefore, had to be interpreted as an utterance of the Gods. Only during the course of human evolution have dreams come to be interpreted in a naturalistic sense.

Or let us take another common dream. The dreamer is going along a path that leads him into a wood. After a while he realises that he has lost his way and cannot go any further.

He tries to do so, but the path comes to an end and trees block the way. He begins to feel uneasy.

Now in ordinary consciousness this dream is easily taken at its face value. But if on thinking over it we forget all naturalistic associations, the spiritual world will say to us: This confusion you have met with is in your own thoughts. In waking consciousness, however, people are often loth to admit how confused their thinking is and how easily they reach a point where they can make no progress but only go round in a circle. This inclination is particularly characteristic of our present civilisation. People consider themselves enlightened thinkers, but in reality they dance around in a circle with their thoughts—either about conventional trivialities or about atoms, which are intellectual constructions of their own. In ordinary consciousness, naturally, they are not disposed to admit this.

In a series of symbolical pictures the dream brings out a man's true nature, and it is spiritual beings who are speaking through it. When anyone takes his dream experience in the right way, his self-knowledge will be greatly enhanced.

Another common human characteristic is that people allow themselves to be led by their instincts and impulses to do what is most congenial to them. For example, they find pleasure in doing something or other, but they are not ready to admit that they are doing it for their own satisfaction. They invent some way of interpreting it differently for their ordinary consciousness—they say perhaps that they are doing it for anthroposophical or occult or esoteric reasons, connected with a high mission or something of that sort. With this kind of self-justification they cover up—and this occurs with extraordinary frequency—an endless amount of all that rules and rages in the depths of our animal life. A dream—which wishes to reveal through symbolical pictures the forces which really hold sway even in the soul and spirit of the dreamer—may present a picture of the man pursued by wild beasts and trying vainly to escape. We shall interpret truly the moral significance of such a dream, not by looking at its outward events, but by accepting the self-knowledge it offers us. We have to recognise it as a warning to search for the inner truth about our own nature and to consider whether this does not resemble—if only slightly—animal instinct rather than what we ideally conjure up.

Hence it is possible for dreams to warn people in countless ways and to set them right. When a dream is related in the true way to the higher world, it can have a guiding influence on a man's life, and then, when the stage of conscious Imagination is reached, one can see how the dream, which at first naturally offers even to Imaginative knowledge pictures drawn from the sense-world, is metamorphosed entirely into moral-spiritual happenings.

Thus we see how the dream can be said to lead ordinary consciousness into the spiritual world, if only it is taken in the right way. But I have said also that on raising ourselves through Imagination to the spiritual world, we are not in the same state of soul as during our life here on Earth. In this life, I stand here, the table is there outside me; there is a physical gap between me and the table. The moment I enter the spiritual world, this separation ceases. I no longer stand here with the table over there; it is as if my whole being were spreading out over the table and the table were taking me into itself. In the spiritual world we sink right into whatever we perceive. Hence our experience, either in dreams or consciously in Imagination, should not be related merely to our inner life, but we can speak in a spiritual-scientific sense if we say with the poet that the whole world is woven out of dreams. It is certainly not woven out of the play of atoms, which is a dream of the scientists, but out of what I have described as the "chaos" of the Greeks, out of the weaving of our dreams and of our conscious Imagination. I have called it both subjective and objective, for the world is not woven purely subjectively; but we have to explain certain aspects of the world as being woven out of dreams.

For example, if we are looking at a seed, we should not be content to explain it by the laws of physics and chemistry. A scientist who sees nothing more than those laws in a seed, or in an embryo, cannot possibly explain them; for nature is dreaming in seed and embryo—their very essence is the weaving life of a dream. Take the seed of a plant—in it a dream is living and weaving. You can never enter into this with the intellect, for that is limited to nature's laws; you must approach it with the human faculty which lives otherwise in a dream or in conscious Imagination.

The same kind of dreaming that lives thus in the seed is active also in our whole organism throughout our life on Earth. Hence we should not look in our organism merely for the working of chemical and physical forces. When a man is there before us physically, we have to look upon him in his external physical form as a being who is living just for a time in the physical world of the senses. Behind him lives something else, invisible to the eye, inaudible to the ear, in so far as these are physical. But it can be perceived in Imagination, and also in what can be experienced in the unconscious Imagination of a dream. In the whole of a man's body nature is dreaming. Nature's way of thinking is not like man's intellectual thinking—it is a dreaming. Out of this dreaming the forces of our digestion and of our growth are guided, and everything is given form.

When we look back in earthly existence we generally start from this age—what shall we call this age of ours? We could take one of its symptoms and call it the age of the typewriter. Thus we go back from this age of the typewriter to the time when printing was first introduced; and going still further back we come perhaps to the time of the Romans, to the time of the Greeks, and then we arrive at the age in the East from which the Vedic records come. We are then left with no external documents. Many treasures have been excavated from the tombs of the Egyptian kings, but we still come at last to a time with no records, where we have to rely on Imaginative and Inspired spiritual knowledge. There we meet with a frontier beyond which, for ordinary consciousness, the past is vague, very much as sleep lies beyond the dream. By going back in this way through the temporal evolution of the world, we come in fact to that dream-veil we can experience every night.

If we reach that point with conscious Imagination, the further past lights up in a spiritual way. But it appears different from the world we learn about intellectually and from ancient records. This remote past in world-evolution, lying behind a veil of dreams, reveals man in direct connection with divine Spirits. He is himself still a divine soul-being; and the divine-spiritual Beings, whose destiny does not include entering an earthly body, meet together with him while he awaits his incarnation on earth.

When, therefore, we look back through history to this veil of chaos, to the dream-veil of which we have been speaking during the last few days, we see the divine Spirits foregathering with the still spiritual souls of men destined to dwell on Earth.

Moreover, we shall see how these things, connected as they are with human evolution, are at the same time connected with cosmic evolution. Where in a remote past this veil appears to Inspired Imagination, we see, too, how within cosmic evolution—of which we shall have to speak more precisely—the Moon, previously united with the Earth, detaches itself and goes out into cosmic space, there to circle the Earth. Thus we gaze back on a dream-veil, a veil of Imagination, and looking through it we find the Earth united with the Moon, and human beings in direct contact with divine-spiritual Beings. When this dream-veil appears to the retrospective gaze of Imagination, we perceive the momentous cosmic event of the Moon, in a quite different form, sliding out of the Earth and going forth into cosmic space as a separate body. So we look further back to the evolution of the Earth, of mankind, and of the world, when these were all united with the Moon. Man was already there, but as a being of soul and spirit only.

As we gaze further and further back, we find no epoch in cosmic evolution when man was not there, at least in some primal form. So that, from the standpoint of Spiritual Science, we cannot say that for millions of years the Earth was evolving merely inorganically or with creatures of a lower order, with man emerging only after that. We find man in a

different form connected at every stage with that cosmic
evolution to which we look back when, behind the veil of
chaos and the dream, we can rise through conscious Imagination to that which appears to us as the divine-spiritual
essence of the world.

As I have said, when we look at a seed or anything in an
embryonic state, Imaginative cognition reveals in it the weaving of a dream. We see how something real, though expressed
in dream-pictures, holds sway over the material part of the
seed. Anyone able to perceive the spiritual in the world will
find it everywhere, though in a great variety of forms. It is
precisely the spiritual that goes through the most varied metamorphoses. And when we have thoroughly grasped how in
the seed of a plant, in the embryo of an animal, this real
dream-weaving prevails, we are justified in asking : How is
it, then, with the apparently dead world of the minerals?
If here we look out of the window or go along the street, we
see the bare hills, a world that seems entirely lifeless, and the
question at once arises : If in any plant seed we pick up there
is a dream-picture ruling, how is it with these rocky mountainous masses, and with all the lifeless substance that forms
the ground we tread on in the physical world? If in the
plants we see the ruling of spirit, which in the weaving of a
dream seizes with comparative ease upon the material element, so in the same way through Imaginative cognition we
find the spiritual in these rocky masses, but here the spiritual
consists of individual spiritual beings.

These spiritual beings, however, are in a state not of
dreaming but of deep sleep. When you look at these rocks
and hills you must not think of them as permeated by a slum-
bering amorphous mist; you should think of individual
spiritual beings sleeping there. Presently we shall see how
these spiritual beings have come into existence through having
been split off from higher beings with a higher consciousness.
We shall see how they themselves, having in their present state
only a sleep-consciousness, are the result of that separation,

and how these elemental beings are asleep everywhere out there in the inanimate world. When we walk over this mountainous mass of rock, we should be aware that all around us there slumbers the creative weaving of the spirit in concrete form. And when we enter further into the sleeping of the spirit-weaving forms in the lifeless world, we become aware in these elemental beings of a certain mood. Imagination shows us these beings, but it is Inspiration that teaches us about their mood. In these elementals of the mountains, the rocks, and the soil, there lives what we can discover in ourselves when we are waiting for something with justified expectation. The weaving and creating of soul and spirit in the seemingly lifeless rocks is permeated by this same expectant mood.

In fact, these beings are waiting to awake from deep sleep into a state of dreaming. We learn this through Inspiration, and more particularly when we enter right into these beings through Intuition. All that confronts us out there, in those hills, is expecting that one day it will be able to dream, and so with dream-consciousness to take hold of earthly substance that is ground down into lifeless matter, and from these rocks and hills to conjure forth once more as embryos, as seeds, living plants. It is indeed these beings who bring before our souls a wonderful magic of nature, a creating from out of the spirit.

And so, as we go about here among these rocks and look at them in the physical light they reflect, they can reveal to us, not in any symbolical sense but as real knowledge, how they are now sleeping, how in the future they will be dreaming, and how, later still, they will come to the fully awake life of elemental nature-beings, who will one day become beings of pure spirit.

The physical material in a plant is still in a condition accessible to the dream-weaving of the spirit. In the rocks, matter is crumbling away. Looking back with Imagination and Inspiration, we realise how everything lifeless has arisen from the living. It is when the living becomes lifeless that the sleeping spirituality can sink into it. This sleeping spirit waits in the lifeless until it can wake into dreams and lead over the lifeless into cosmic embryonic life.

Now the various parts of the Earth show in different ways this sleep of spiritual beings in the mountains, in the firm crust of the Earth. It might be said : The sleep of beings awaiting their future is different in regions such as this from their sleep in other parts of the Earth. Here in Penmaenmawr we find that the particular configuration of the Earth, and the historical character of the rocks, enable these sleeping beings to rise to the aeriform, to interweave even with the light, while in other parts of the Earth this has long ceased to be so. Thus it is that here, if we look on the weaving as due not to the aerial atmosphere alone, but to the prevailing soul-atmosphere, which permeates the air just as the human soul permeates a man's body, then in Penmaenmawr we find that this soul-element in the atmosphere is different from elsewhere. I will give just one example to make this clear.

Suppose that in a certain region Imaginative cognition exerts itself to call up an Imagination of what is really going on there. This Imagination may be more or less easy or difficult to hold on to, for the possibility of retaining an Imagination in consciousness varies in different regions. Here we are in a region where Imaginations continue for a remarkably long time and so are able to become very vivid.

The wise men of the Druids, or others of that kind, sought out regions for their temples and sanctuaries where the conditions were such as to allow Imaginations to remain and not immediately to vanish away like clouds. Hence we can understand how it was that such centres for the holy places of the Druids were still sought for up to comparatively recent times. In this region it has always been felt that the difficulty of holding an Imagination is not so great as in other places. Everything, of course, has a light side and a shadow side. When an Imagination remains, Inspiration is made harder, though it gains in strength. Because of that, whatever the spiritual world has to say in this place streams down with —one might say—greater intensity, but in words which are weightier and more difficult.

Therefore, even where the spiritual is in question, differentiations are to be found throughout the Earth. A map might be drawn indicating the places where, for Imaginative consciousness, there is no difficulty in holding Imaginations. Those regions where they soon pass away could be given a different colour, and we should get an extraordinarily interesting map of the Earth. For the prevailing character of soul-atmosphere here, we should need a particularly strong colour—a sparkling, shining colour, full of life.

Hence I fully believe that those taking part in this lecture-course will be able to perceive here something of what I would call the esoteric mood of the elementals. It looks in at the windows, meets us on our walks, in fact is present everywhere in a quite special way. I am particularly grateful to the organisers of the course for having thus chosen a spot where the esoteric may be said to meet one at every turn. It does so indeed in other places, but not with the same ease and directness. So I am especially thankful for the choice of this place, out of many possible for the holding of a course such as this. From the point of view of the subjects discussed, this course may be said to take its place, in a wonderfully beautiful way, in the whole evolution of the Anthroposophical Movement.

It will be clear from the descriptions I have been giving you that between the physical world of the senses and the spiritual, supersensible world, there is a barrier which with a certain rightness we call the Threshold of the spiritual world.

I have already pointed out in various ways how necessary it is that we should be able to cross this Threshold, and we have still to speak about it in greater detail. But you will have gathered already from my lectures that in older periods of human evolution this crossing of the Threshold was a rather different matter from what it is at the present day. In those ancient times people were able to cross in another way because even by day their consciousness was dreamlike, but for that very reason more alive to the supersensible. Thus, in the way I have pictured, they passed the Guardian of the Threshold half-consciously, dreamily, both on going to sleep and on waking.

Here we can see a transition from men of an older type, with little freedom, to those who were becoming increasingly free. This former determinism was bound up with the fact that on going to sleep, and on awaking, men had some perception of the Guardian of the Threshold, who stood there giving warning. Now, in place of this unfree situation, we have the incapacity of present-day consciousness to see into the spiritual world, which signifies an increasing freedom : herein lies a principle of human progress.

Hence we can say that, looked at from the spiritual world, people have lost a great deal precisely because in the course of their evolution they have had to be led towards freedom. What has been lost, however, must be regained, in the way that Anthroposophy, for example, would show. And now is the historical point of time when a striving to regain what has been lost must begin.

But everywhere, among people of very various kinds, there still rises up something inherited from an earlier age, when man's relation to the spiritual world was different. So that to-day, in the consciousness of those given up to intellectualism, there is a strict frontier set up, as a rule, between what they experience in the world of the senses and what lies beyond in the spiritual world. The frontier is in fact so rigorously maintained that even enlightened spirits are unwilling to admit the possibility of crossing it.

In my brief sketch of the way into the supersensible world, I have indicated that it is possible to cross the frontier and to enter that world in full consciousness. But as a relic from the time when a man entered the spiritual world in a more instinctive, unconscious way, and even in his day-consciousness had more in him of the spiritual world, there still rises up into his evolution to-day a certain heritage from the past. And this is something we must imperatively understand through conscious spiritual cognition. For, if not rightly understood, it manifests itself in many deceptive ways, and in these matters such errors can become very dangerous. Hence in the course

of these lectures, intended to describe the evolution of man
and of the world, I must speak about this question of a boun-
dary, where what was natural and taken for granted among
the people of former epochs re-appears to-day, and can lead
to dangerous illusions in those who have not the requisite
clear knowledge for dealing with it.

Among these phenomena, situated for ordinary consciousness at the frontier between the sense-world and the supersensible, are *visions*. I mean the visions where, in a state of
hallucination more or less controlled by the person concerned,
pictures arise which have quite definite forms and colours—
they may even seem to speak—but correspond to nothing external. For normal perception, the object is outside; the image,
in a shadowy way within; and a person is perfectly conscious
of how the shadowy, conceptual image is related to the external world. The vision arises of itself, claiming to be a
reality on its own account. A person subject to such visions
becomes incapable of estimating rightly what reality there is
in the pictures which appear before him without his initiative.

How, then, do visions come about? They come about
because the human being still possesses the capacity for carrying over into his waking world what he experiences during
sleep, and of bringing it into conceptual form just as he does
with his sense-perceptions. Whether, after perceiving a clock
that exists physically for the senses, I make an inner picture
of it, or whether, after experiencing in a dream the form
and inner reality of an external object, I wake up and make
a picture of my experience, the only difference between the
two processes is that I am in control of one of them—hence
the image of it is more shadowy and flat—while the other
process is outside my control. In the latter case I carry nothing of the real present into my conceptual life, but something
experienced when the soul was outside in a past—perhaps
long past—sleep, and out of this dream-experience I build up
a vision.

In an earlier age of human evolution, when the relation
of people both to the physical world and to the spiritual world
was ruled by instinct, such visions were perfectly natural; it is

human progress that has made them the uncontrolled, illusory things they are to-day. We must therefore be quite clear that modern man lacks something : when he has some experience in the spiritual world during sleep and is returning to the physical world, he no longer hears the warning of the Guardian of the Threhold : "All that you have experienced in the spiritual world you should note well and carry back to the physical world." If he does carry it back, he will know what is contained in the vision. But if the vision appears to him only in the physical world, without his realising that he has brought it back from the spiritual world, so that he fails to understand what it really is, then he is without guidance, and at the mercy of illusion where his visionary experience is concerned. So we can say : Visions come about because a man carries over unawares his sleep-experience into his waking life, and in his waking life he then forms conceptions of the experiences—conceptions which are much richer in content than the ordinary shadowy ones, and these he builds up into vivid visions complete with colour and sound.

Another thing that comes about is this. A man carries over into his life of sleep the feelings and perceptions of the kind he has in physical life. Then, when he is in the act of carrying this over into the open sea of sleep-life, he is warned to be careful not to do anything foolish. If the sleep is very light—a far more common condition in ordinary life than is realised, for we are often just a little asleep when walking about quite normally, and we ought to be more aware of this—we may then, without noticing it, carry over the Threshold our everyday faculty of perception. Then arise those obscure feelings, as if one were inwardly watching something happening in the future, either to oneself or to someone else, and we have a *premonition*. Thus, whereas a *vision* comes about when experience during sleep is carried down into waking life and the threshold is crossed unconsciously, *premonition* comes about when we are in a light sleep without realising it and, thinking we are awake, carry over the Threshold, again ignoring the Guardian, our daytime experience. This, however, lies so deep down in the subconscious that it is not noticed. We are, of course, at all times connected with the whole world; and if we could draw this knowledge up out of the subconscious, we should be able to draw up much else also.

You will now see how, because these legacies from the evolutionary past can still be experienced, visions arise on one side of the Threshold, premonitions on the other. But a man may also halt at the Threshold and still not notice the Guardian. There may then be moments when inwardly, in his soul, he is as if he were enchanted. But the word "enchanted" does not quite meet the case, for he is not enchanted in the sense we generally associate with the term—it is rather that his attitude of soul undergoes a change. When he comes to the Threshold in such a way that he still perceives what is in the physical world while already perceiving what is in the supersensible, he experiences something which is widespread in certain regions of the Earth—*second sight,* a half-conscious experience at the Threshold. Hence to sum up these legacies from the past, these phenomena in a man's life when his consciousness is dimmed, we have those appearing on this side of the Threshold as *visions;* those appearing beyond the Threshold as *premonitions;* those actually at the Threshold as *second sight.*

To-morrow I shall have to speak in greater detail of the characteristics of these three regions, going on from these to describe the worlds dimly indicated by vision, premonition and second sight—worlds which new knowledge will have to bring into the full clarity of enhanced consciousness.

VII

The Interplay of Various Worlds

In human life there is a perpetual interplay between the supersensible world and the world of the senses; and I have also referred to extreme cases where the two worlds—or really all three—play into one another without a man contributing anything to it through his own development. To-day we shall be speaking about human examples of interplay between the various worlds. I will first describe the ordinary sleep-walking type, then the Jacob Boehme type, and finally the type represented by Swedenborg.

The relation of these three types to one another is such that each may be said to indicate, as if by a universally valid experiment, how human evolution is connected with the evolution of the world as a whole. This too I would bring to your notice in what I have to say.

In studying these three types of men, who enter and leave the spiritual world without fully recognising the presence of the Guardian at the Threshold, we find indeed that all three —the sleep-walker type, the Jacob Boehme type and the Swedenborg type—have a way of perceiving the supersensible world—or, as is particularly true of the sleep-walker, are active therein—which is different from the way opened by Imaginative, Inspired, and Intuitive cognition. This derives from the fact that when anyone enters the spiritual world— and everyone does so, if only unconsciously, whenever he goes to sleep—all things, as I have already pointed out, become different from what they are in the physical world.

Three features of the supersensible world, above all, are the opposite of those in the physical world. This contrast has such a strong effect on human beings and is so disturbing to all they hold true, right, salutary and so on in the physical world that, given the present earthly condition of soul and body, people should never be transplanted suddenly into the supersensible world without due preparation. Hence in my book, *Knowledge of the Higher Worlds*, I have laid particular stress on the necessity for the right sort of preparation. It is described there in such a way that anyone who follows the directions will be prepared in all respects for entering the supersensible world in the right way. All the three types I am speaking of to-day, however, enter not because of preparation but through their destiny, and their destiny, their karma, protects them from any dangers. Indeed, through their karma they are made acquainted with many things concerning mankind which can otherwise be known only through Imaginative, Inspired and Intuitive cognition.

First of all, in the spiritual-supersensible world, all weight, all gravity ceases. When really within the spiritual world, one is never in anything that can be weighed, but in the imponderable. The first conscious experience there is like the feeling we might have in the physical world if the ground were falling away under our feet, and we had to hold firm through our own inner forces.

So you must imagine how, if we wish really to enter the spiritual world, we are bound to have this feeling of the ground being spirited away from under us, and how with no gravity to rely on, we have to maintain ourselves in free space by the strength within us.

The second thing that ceases in the supersensible is all that we have as sense-perception in the physical world. To put it briefly: in the supersensible world light ceases and one finds oneself in darkness. But that is not the whole story, for in reality it is not only light·that ceases; light ceases in the physical world for the blind, who still possess other senses. But in the science of the spirit the word light often embraces not only light and colour, but everything audible, tangible or perceptible as warmth, and so on. In the supersensible world, all this ceases. And one can imply this by referring simply to what for most people is their chief sense-experience, and so by saying: Where there was light, everything becomes dark.

The third thing to be met in the spiritual world—and we must strive to feel this in its full reality—is emptiness in place of fullness. Here in the physical world there is generally something to touch, and when there is nothing else you are still surrounded by the air. Everywhere is fullness. In the spiritual world it is just the opposite; everywhere is emptiness. Hence we can say : In the physical world of the senses, the prevailing experiences are of the ponderable, of light in the physical sense, which includes everything experienced by the senses; and thirdly, fulness. Whereas in the spiritual world there prevail the imponderable; darkness in which a man must provide his own light from what he has developed inwardly during his evolution; and emptiness he has to fill for higher consciousness with the reality he absorbs by entering into other spiritual beings through Intuition.

Now when a man, through instinctive destiny, is led out of the ponderable into the realm where the imponderable prevails, he is seized upon by forces from beyond the Earth. Anyone going about the physical Earth, or even when lying down, is always subject to the laws of gravity. If he were to escape from them for a few minutes, the opposing force, counter-gravity, comes into play. He then experiences within himself a force dragging him away from the Earth, instead of chaining him to it. This is the same force that comes from the Moon, besides the light it reflects.

When, therefore, anyone is going about on Earth, he is exposed in normal life to the force of gravity which draws him down and holds him fast to the Earth. If through his karma, which is then linked with the nature-forces holding sway in him, this earthly gravity is withrawn at certain moments, so that Moon-forces can begin to act on him as counter-gravity, then, though he is still asleep, he starts to wander about. He is then exposed to the forces that govern his physical and etheric bodies—forces which are related not only to forces reflected back from the Moon in light but to many other forces streaming from Moon to Earth. These forces pull on the man; they are always trying to draw him away from the Earth. In the moment when, instead of being in the grip of earthly gravity, he is seized upon by the forces of counter-gravity, coming from the Moon and working against the earthly forces, he may wander about in the moonstruck way of the somnambulist. The forces holding sway in a man at this moment are quite different from the normal earthly ones; but this applies only to the present day. These forces are now found only in the somnambulist, and are abnormal. Call to him by his earthly name when under the influence of the Moon he is wandering about on a roof—and he will fall. He thus comes immediately into the realm of Earth-forces; but in other epochs men were not given names such as they have to-day, and the temporary condition of the sleepwalker was then normal. Anyone who looks right into the matter will see that earthly man, in his so-called normal life to-day, is bound up with the forces of the Earth. The moonstruck person, however, points us away from human evolution to world-evolution, and in fact to that epoch when world-evolution was Moon-evolution.

The moment a man enters the realm of Moon-evolution, he behaves as though he did not live in the physical realm of the Earth at all, but in the astral world, though the astral enters into the physical and makes use of the physical body. And that which the astral develops physically in this way was at one time Moon-evolution. We are reminded that astral activity in the physical was once world-evolution—Moon-evolution—and will be so again. But then a man will be able in full consciousness to walk up steeply sloping surfaces, as flies can do to-day. This is an indication of what will come about in the future during the Jupiter-evolution. Thus, if we rightly understand the somnambulist, we can study the physical picture he presents, as if nature herself were giving us a demonstration of what we experienced during our Moon-existence—not, certainly, in a physical body of flesh, but in an infinitely finer substance—and of what we shall experience again when we learn to master physical substance quite consciously, during the Jupiter-evolution. So this sleep-walking state points both to the past and to the future in the evolution of the world.

In this connection we are concerned entirely with human beings whom we can call Moon-men, who in certain moments of their life become somnambulists. But this sleep-walking behaviour, this going about in the imponderable, can be accomplished spiritually, in full consciousness, if at the same time one has sufficient strength to keep perfectly still. The somnambulist follows the impulses of the Moon-forces; he gives himself over unconsciously to them and makes every movement to which they impel him. But anyone who goes through this experience with exact, conscious clairvoyance refrains from any such movements; he keeps still. The effect is that the movements undergo a metamorphosis in him and become Intuitions. Conscious Intuition, therefore, the highest development of strict clairvoyance, actually consists in arresting the actions which a sleep-walker is instinctively compelled by the Moon-forces to perform. Anyone who brings about this metamorphosis does not give himself up to the physical forces of the Moon but holds them in check within himself. Thus he is enabled to devote himself intuitively to the relevant spirituality; that is, he attains to Intuition.

Hence it is really very good to study in these Moon-men how, on the one hand, man is related to world-evolution, and on the other how the somnambulist and the exact clairvoyant are opposites. Whereas it is instinctive people who are the moonstruck sleep-walkers, exact clairvoyants are intuitive seers who, refraining from action, hold their own against the Moon. That is what we are shown at this point in the relation of man to the world.

Now the second of the three types of men of whom I am speaking to-day is exemplified in Jacob Boehme. He was so fully endowed a man that at certain moments of his life, as though through his natural destiny, his karma, he was able while completely awake to conjure up before him, instead of the sunlit world, dark space. From what I have already said you will be clear that here it is a question not only of the darkness which is absence of light, but of the blotting out of everything perceived by the senses. It was possible for Jacob Boehme, under certain conditions during his life, to be faced by darkness in place of light, by silence and stillness instead of the various sounds in the world, and instead of warmth by something—equally unlike warmth or cold—we might call anti-warmth, and so on. So that, if through Inspiration one had examined these states of his, without experiencing them oneself, one would have had to say that Jacob Boehme, instead of having sunlit space around him, was at certain times faced by complete darkness.

People who have this experience without being conscious of it—who are, that is, in a light sleep though still feeling themselves to be in the ordinary sunlit world—have what is called second-sight : and this is what Jacob Boehme had in its most pronounced form. Only, in his case, it was applied less to individual particulars on the Earth and more to the constitution of the Earth as a whole. What, then, was his vision?

Now picture this to yourselves. When other people have before them the light of the Sun, Jacob Boehme had— precisely from the point where the visual rays of the eyes meet, on looking at some object far away or near, or from behind the point where a barrier arises when we fold our right hand over our left and shut ourselves off from the outer world—there Jacob Boehme was faced by darkness and silence in respect of all his senses. Imagine this complete darkness! There is a physical picture closely corresponding to it. When you stand before a mirror, you don't see what is behind it— only what is in front. Spiritually, it is the same for anyone who sees in Jacob Boehme's way. The darkness behind creates something in front like a mirror, in which one sees reflected the earthly world in its spirituality. Thus, if you were of the Jacob Boehme type, at certain moments in your life you would look into darkness, and, because this darkness rayed back to you the spiritual life of the Earth, you would behold the spiritual constitution of the Earth and the course of its existence.

It was a powerful second-sight that Jacob Boehme had. Another man may have certain moments in h s life when he is faced by darkness which shuts out the physical light, enabling him to look into the spiritual. Then, if he understands how to make the right use of this spiritual mirror, which consists simply in the existence of the darkness, then, through the inner communications between all earthly things, deeds and even thoughts, he will be able when in Europe to perceive a friend in America. For what we perceive with our physical eyes and senses results, above all, from the action of the Sun. But there are also hidden workings of the Sun, active in everything—in minerals, plants, animals, and also in human beings. While you may be in Europe, yet through these hidden workings of the Sun within you, you are in communication with a friend in far-off America, in whom these same forces are active.

These communications have karmic effects. Many a person has had his destiny for marriage, love, friendship, linked with someone in America, perhaps, who was unknown to him at that time. In this working of karma on Earth the hidden forces of the Sun are active; they are made visible there, as though in a mirror.

This applies particularly to people leading isolated lives on islands, in mountain valleys, or in other places favourable in this respect, and the fact that second-sight is fairly common in such places is because persons leading secluded lives respond more readily than others to these inner communications and are able to spread a partial darkness around them in life. Hence the Scottish and the Westphalian second-sight, and the second-sight in a secluded valley of Alsace so beautifully described by Oberlin. Thus such things appear in special districts of the Earth. Where they are genuine, like those hidden effects of the Sun of which I have just spoken, they need to be judged quite differently from the way in which they usually are judged in our materialistic age.

Certain people nowadays, proud of their cleverness, discuss whether there ever was a King Arthur, whether he was a real or a legendary figure. But those who can look more deeply into the matter will speak differently. And for them, anyone who doubts whether King Arthur ever lived is himself far more legendary than King Arthur! Take a modern scholar who denies the existence of Arthur—well, he is physically present among us, but in fact he belongs far more to the realm of sagas and legends than King Arthur does, at least in the opinion of those who can see into the truth of these things.

Hence we can say of people who have second-sight, the gift manifest to the highest degree in Jacob Boehme, that they are in a special sense Sun-men. Just as we normally see the effects of the Sun in the external world, these Sun-men are inwardly permeated by the Sun's hidden forces. And just as our first type was seen to consist of Moon-men, the second type consists of Sun-men, like Jacob Boehme with his second-sight. They are Sun-men who through their natural karma bear within them something which is abnormal to-day, but for that very reason thoroughly in accordance with reality; for what is abnormal to-day has been, at some time, quite normal.

Thus, by realising what men with second-sight are able to perceive, by bringing home to ourselves the nature of the Sun's hidden forces, by which these Sun-men are permeated, we are able to say : This living in the hidden effects of the Sun, now abnormal, was normal at an earlier stage of the Earth's evolution, and it will be normal again. It was normal during the period which as Sun-evolution preceded Earth-evolution. It was normal then for men everywhere to look into darkness as if into a mirror, in order to have the spiritual reflected back to them. The whole Earth went through that stage of evolution which made man, in his tenuous, volatile materiality at that time, a Sun-man. Consciousness was then very dim.

This condition will come again. A man will then be able to penetrate with full consciousness the darkness around him, producing by his own efforts a reflected image of the whole world. By that time we shall have arrived at the Venus-evolution, a future stage of Earth-evolution.

Persons wishing to acquire second-sight must cast off their coarse perceptions and sensibility, and the sensations they receive from the physical in their environment; they must draw a free sensibility out of themselves. This can also be arrived at inwardly, though not without danger. It can be done by anyone who fixes his gaze—I am not advising this, simply giving you facts—on some glittering object, so to induce a state of fascination. In this way outer sensibility is weakened, inner sensibility is encouraged, and second-sight is evoked. In ancient times, under certain circumstances, second-sight was evoked quite systematically. Stories of this refer to a "magic mirror" : this was in fact an instrument designed to fascinate and so to damp down outer sensation, thereby calling up inner sensation as its polar opposite. A physical mirror was thus used for calling up a spiritual reflection. The important thing was not what was seen in the physical mirror; the physical mirror merely drove away all outer sensation and inner sensation was evoked. That is how the belief arose that in the magic mirror itself the feelings, the thoughts, and so on, of distant friends could be seen. In reality the person saw the state of soul brought about in himself by the ordinary mirror.

Anyone who elicits this kind of seeing sees actual realities. He sees the spiritual activity that goes on in the kingdoms of nature, and he is, as it were, united with everything on Earth that is Sun-like.

In order really to understand Jacob Boehme's writings, one must take their whole content as deriving from a complicated, wonderful second-sight.

Another personality, Paracelsus, was constituted in a similar yet somewhat different way. Sensation in his case was combined with greater intellectual power; hence he always interpreted the pictures revealed to him by second-sight. When we reflect intellectually about physical, sense-perceptible things, we do not change them, for the intellect is powerless in face of the physical; but it is not powerless in face of anything seen in a mirror in the way described. To perceive the inner constitution of the world so purely in terms of second-sight is possible only for someone like Jacob Boehme, who was able to surrender himself quite selflessly to external things. The unending love with which he looked upon all things, and which made itself felt in his whole way of grasping the reflected images of the spiritual in the world, speaks in almost every line he wrote. So these reflections remained for him in the utmost purity as a kind of Imaginations of the spiritual in the world.

With Paracelsus, all these things went through a change in accordance with his strong intellectual bent. Hence they are reflected images given a different form. Even from a physical mirror you can learn that what it reflects can go through a change—you have only to look at your face in a concave mirror. You would certainly be loth to have a face as you see it there! That is more or less what intellectuality does to the reflecting surface into which one looks—if one is an intellectual such as Paracelsus. By this means, however, one pentrates more deeply into the inner forces.

Thus Jacob Boehme, beholding all things with his truly sublime love, became a contemplative observer; whereas Paracelsus, concentrating more on the inner forces, and distorting the mirror-images he was dealing with, approached nearer to the healing forces that lie within things as hidden Sun-forces.

When anyone learns to master consciously the hidden Sun-forces, so that he does not use the outspread darkness for seeing reflected images but carries into the darkness the inner light kindled in soul and spirit through meditation and concentration; when he becomes able to fill with inner soul-forces the space otherwise lit up by the physical Sun so that he can illuminate it with the light of his own soul and spirit, then indeed conscious Imagination arises. This conscious Imagination, that can be evoked in the way we have learnt to do on the path of knowledge, is the source of what Jacob Boehme, as a Sun-man, has recorded to a certain extent unconsciously in his writings, and with less mastery of the world of ideas and so on.

And so, just as Intuition arises when the secret forces of the Moon in a man are held fast, and not expressed in somnambulistic wanderings, so the mirror-images conjured up by the

Sun-forces out of spiritual darkness are changed to conscious Imagination.

While the sleep-walking type lives in the forces of the Moon, and the Jacob Boehme type in those of the Sun, so a third type lives in the conditions of warmth and cold always present in the space around the Earth. In normal life people grow accustomed to the prevailing temperature. But there is a certain delicate, intimate sensitivity that becomes independent of the external warmth or cold, and on the contrary is very susceptible to the hidden workings of heat and cold which permeate the space surrounding and penetrating the Earth. A faculty of this kind for perceiving these hidden workings was acquired at a certain time in his life by Swedenborg. Anyone wishing to make a study of the mysterious side of Swedenborg's life will gradually come to see clearly that this susceptibility appeared in him at a certain age, for up to that time he had been a distinguished representative of the official science of his day: his writings in this field are very numerous. They were not all published at the time, but now a society of Swedish scholars is preparing an edition of his scientific works in many volumes. Swedenborg will certainly give these scholars some hard nuts to crack! They are obliged to admit that his works prove him to have been one of the greatest geniuses of his age, but at a certain moment of his life he became clairvoyant—which, in the opinion of those editing his officially recognised works, is another word for half-witted.

Now we must turn our attention rather to this higher vision developed by Swedenborg after he had made himself familiar with the rest of the knowledge recognised in his day. We must examine more closely the reasons for his thus becoming "half-witted" in the eyes of official learning.

On looking deeply into Swedenborg's personality, we find that he "lost his senses" because in his fortieth year he developed an overwhelming love for all that he had learnt up to that time. There can hardly be anyone who has loved pure knowledge as much as Swedenborg came to love it. It was this love for knowledge that enabled him at a certain point in his life to look in his own way into the spiritual world, and to become susceptible to the hidden effects of warmth and cold in surrounding space.

These hidden effects of warmth and cold come neither from Moon nor from Sun, but chiefly from a heavenly body that sends very unassuming rays into interplanetary space— from Saturn. These modest rays carry the hidden forces which, at a certain time of his life, permeated Swedenborg particularly. On this account he developed a capacity for perceiving, instead of the fullness by which we are surrounded in the world of the senses, emptiness—and to this, one day, he became sensitive. He made no effort to become so; it arose instinctively. Nor did he undergo any training such as I have described in the book *Knowledge of the Higher Worlds;* this sensitivity dawned within him like a delicate higher instinct. And so he became able to look into the world—not a physical world—which is perceptible only when we have entered into the conditions of warmth and cold that stream as rays from Saturn through interplanetary space. Thus he developed a very individual form of vision.

If you read what Swedenborg has recorded as the results of this vision, it really seems almost like an etherealised, subtilised, earthly experience. The spiritual beings he sees, Angels, Archangels, and so on, certainly move with the freedom of the imponderable, but almost in the manner of earthly beings. We may ask whether the world he was looking at was real, or whether he was simply projecting into the void what he drew from his own inner resources. No—the truth is quite different. Besides the world into which we look with our physical senses, and besides the second world we can experience, the etheric world, we are surrounded by a purely spiritual world. In this spiritual world there are spiritual beings who have never descended to Earth, beings leading a life of movement and activity. These beings have to send their influence into earthly life; hence they impart to the etheric element of the Earth their activity in the purely spiritual world. We can describe it in this way. The Earth is surrounded, permeated, by its etheric element, and outside—actually outside space—there is the world of these active spiritual beings which enters into the earthly realm. The Earth is what it is only through the activity of these beings.

This activity rays into the earthly realm, but is rayed back and reflected in the ether of the Earth; and the forces of the ether are actually the etheric realisation of the spiritual above them. When we study the etheric around us on the Earth, we find it permeated with the activity of these spiritual beings in the form of etheric pictures. The actual activity takes place above it or within it. What immediately surrounds us on Earth is the activity that is projected back into the ether of the Earth. It is just as if a looking-glass were not only to reflect images but gradually to develop an activity of its own. Spiritual activity is rayed back from the Earth into the ether, and this activity is really a projection of spiritual activity.

Just as Jacob Boehme saw in a mirror the reflection of what goes on in the human body or in nature, in the way I have described, for Swedenborg the Earth itself was the mirror which threw back to him in the ether the pictures of spiritual activity in the spiritual world. We can say that what he saw is not the spiritual world, or we can equally well say that it is. It is just the realisation of an image reflected by the Earth. It is a true image, but true only as a reflection of the reality that lies behind it.

That is what Swedenborg perceived. In the ether of the Earth he saw how the super-earthly beings develop forces in the ether—forces which play a positive part in human life and also in other forms of life on Earth. These etheric forces are neither Angels nor Archangels, but forces vibrating in the ether. To-day it is abnormal for anyone to see into these hidden etheric forces, which project everywhere into the surrounding ether an etheric image of the higher spiritual archetypes. In an earlier epoch of Earth-evolution, however, this was perfectly normal—in the time which preceded the Sun-evolution and may be called the Saturn age. It was made known at that time that one day we shall experience a Venus age, after which will come the Vulcan age.

In Swedenborg there arose this special kind of vision—the mode of existence once passed through by the Earth; how the Earth revealed itself to the men of that time; and how it will reveal itself in future.

When someone has acquired the capacity for seeing consciously the pictures Swedenborg beheld in the ether; when to the emptiness of world-space he can oppose his own fullness —then, for exact clairvoyance, the beings who were reflected etherically for Swedenborg vanish from etheric vision, and begin to be audible to spiritual hearing, spiritual ears. When they are effaced as visionary pictures, they gradually become Inspirations, sounding into consciousness from out of the spiritual world.

Hence we can say: The unconscious Imagination, rising up in Swedenborg as etheric images, will—if one carefully observes the warnings of the Guardian of the Threshold, which Swedenborg could not do—go through a metamorphosis and reappear as fully conscious astral Inspiration.

Now I have shown you how the more subconscious state of the sleep-walker, the Jacob Boehme type of vision, and the Swedenborg type, are related to what can be striven for consciously as Intuition, Imagination, Inspiration. These have had to be put in a different order to-day because I have been giving a cosmic picture. If this is done in accordance not with names but with the things in themselves, then, if descriptions are given from different points of view, the sequence has to be changed, just as things may often appear in a different order when the perspective is changed. For instance, say I am between two men, with one behind me and the other in front. If I move ahead of the one in front, then I can face them both. So, too, in cosmic space things change in accordance with our point of view.

That is why in my lecture-cycles you find things appearing in a different order according to the various standpoints from which they have to be described. When this is not fully appreciated and anyone persists in an abstract approach, he will say : This does not tally. But the only people who can afford to satisfy the pure intellectualist in this matter are those whose descriptions derive from mere assumptions. Anyone who is describing realities must allow them to appear contradictory, as from different points of view they often can.

VIII

During Sleep and after Death

From what has been said about the relation of sleeping to waking in man, and also about the membering of his organism, it can be seen that in sleep he experiences a profound cleavage in his earthly existence. We know that a distinction has to be made between the part of man which is materially perceptible to the senses, his physical body, and the part that can be seen only through Imagination, his etheric or formative forces body. This formative forces body embraces also the living forces which enable a man to grow, underlie his nutritive processes and generally build him up. As we have seen, the formative forces body includes also the whole system of a man's thoughts. Intermingled with his formative forces body and his physical body are two higher members, which we may call the astral body and the Ego-organisation.

In a man's life during the day these four members of his being are in active inner relationship with one another. But when he passes into the sleeping state, his physical and etheric bodies separate from the Ego and astral body. They remain— if one may put it thus—in bed, while the astral and Ego organisations enter a purely spiritual world. So that, from his falling asleep until he wakes, a man's being is split in two —on the one hand there are his physical organisation and the etheric that holds his world of thought; on the other, the Ego and the astral organisation.

I believe someone in the course of these days has voiced the misgiving : If in sleep a man's whole thought-world remains in the etheric organisation, then he must be unable to carry effectively into the sleeping state the thoughts which he can grasp only while he is awake. This shows a certain anxiety lest wishes for one's fellow-men, for example, or thoughts relating to an absent one, should lose all power because they cannot be taken over into the life of sleep. I should like to reply with a picture.

You are not very likely to have heard of anyone who, wanting to shoot at a target, thought he had to throw his gun at it. While still holding the gun he lets the charge do the work, and you cannot say that nothing reaches the target because the gun remains in the man's hands. It is just the same in the case we are considering. The effects of our thinking life when we are awake do not cease during sleep because the thoughts remain in the physical and etheric bodies. It is particularly important with these subtle matters that we should be precise in our thinking—precise to a degree unnecessary in the physical world, where the things themselves provide immediate corrections. From what has been said in these last few days, however, you will see that a much more intimate relation exists between the physical body and the etheric body than between the etheric body and the astral organisation. For throughout the whole of an earthly life the physical body and the etheric remain together, never separating even when, in sleep, the etheric body and the astral body have to part company.

There is a close connection, on the other hand, between the Ego and the astral organisation, for neither do they ever part from one another during life on Earth. But the connection between the astral and the etheric bodies is looser, and it is there that the split can occur. This has a quite definite effect on a man's earthly life, and also on his life beyond the Earth. In our waking state we give life to our senses through our Ego, and through the astral body to our nervous system; and what is brought about in this way we send down into the etheric and physical bodies, as we must do if we are to live in the physical world. Hence, because everything has to be imprinted into the physical body, in order to become manifest in life from birth or conception until death, a materialist supposes that the physical body can make up the whole of a man's being.

This work of incorporating the experiences of earthly existence into the etheric body and the physical body does not proceed, however, without meeting obstacles and hindrances.

We are never able to send down straight away into the organs of these bodies our experiences and the thoughts embodied in our nervous system, for anything we absorb from the external physical world is at first in a form moulded by that world. If, for example, we perceive something angular, an experience of this angular quality forms itself in our Ego and our astral body. This cannot be taken up immediately into the etheric body, for the etheric body struggles against absorbing anything experienced in the external world of the senses. Imaginative knowledge alone is able to throw light on this situation. No ordinary sense-observation, no material experiment, no intellectual reflection, will help us to a view of this necessary re-forming, re-shaping, of what we perceive with the senses, so as to fit it for living in the etheric body and physical body in such a way that we can separate from it in sleep. It is only when we are able to observe the actual relation between waking and sleeping in earthly man that we come to realise the continuous conflict that goes on in life. Thus—in the case of the crude example already mentioned— if I have to take my experience of an angular object into my etheric and physical bodies, I must first round off its angles and give the object a form suited to those bodies. It has to be completely transformed.

This transforming of anything having as volatile a life as that of the Ego and astral body themselves, and giving it a plastic form capable of living in the etheric body and of continuing its existence as plastic movement in the physical body—this transformation creates an inner struggle not perceived by ordinary consciousness to-day, but anyone who has Imaginative knowledge can perceive it. Generally it lasts two or three days. We have to sleep on an experience for two or often three nights for it to unite with the other experiences already imprinted in the etheric and physical bodies. The dream-world is an actual expression, but only an outward expression, of this struggle. While a man is dreaming, his Ego and his astral body flow into his etheric and physical bodies and come to a sudden stop—as already explained. This check is an expression of the struggle I am now picturing; it goes on for two or three days. Until the experience has been slept upon more than once, it has not gone sufficiently far down into the etheric body, so that where the connection is loose, as it is between astral body and etheric body, a continuous inter-weaving is to be seen.

If we have here the etheric body and the astral is there asleep, then on the verge of waking or of going to sleep a con-tinuous struggle takes place, a movement full of life, ex-pressed outwardly in the dream, but signifying inwardly this weaving of experiences into the etheric and physical bodies. It is only when a man has slept on some experience two or three times—perhaps more often—that the experience is united with the memories already bound up with his etheric and physical bodies. The point is that the experience has to be transformed into memory, which is left lying in bed during sleep, for a memory is essentially the expression in thought of the physi-cal and etheric bodies.

For Imaginative cognition, perceiving this is an extra-ordinarily interesting experience. The very form of its expres-sion is significant. We give our ordinary earthly experiences definite outlines in conformity with natural laws. These laws, however, no longer hold good when the experiences merge with the etheric; everything firmly outlined becomes soft and plastic. Whatever was at rest begins to move; anything angular becomes rounded. Intellectual experience passes over into the experience of the artist.

That is the deeper reason why, in those ancient days when people still had instinctive vision, art was rooted in life in a quite different way from anything we have to-day. Even as late as the Renaissance, in the searching back to earlier art there was still in Raphael and other painters at least a tradi-tion of that conversion of the intellectual into the artistic. For the intellectual loses its form, and takes on the nature of art, directly we rise to the supersensible. The fact that in art to-day people are so strongly inclined to naturalism, wanting models for all their work, shows that they no longer realise its true nature. Humanity must find its way again into the true realm of art.

Human life as I have described it is thus made up in such a way that it is always possible to say : I am experiencing something which will take three days to flow into the etheric body. A day later, the experience of the previous day will flow in. Hence it takes a man two, three, or even four days to complete this uniting of an experience with the etheric body.

Now when a man passes through the gate of death, the etheric body detaches itself from the physical body—something that never happens during earthly life. And now, when the etheric body is free of the physical, all that has been interwoven into the etheric body is gradually dispersed, and this process lasts for about as long—two, three or four days—as the interweaving did. Imagination, which can judge rightly of these matters, shows how during life the physical body holds together, through its resistance, the experiences that have gradually penetrated into the etheric body. When the physical body is laid aside at death, it can be seen how in the first few days afterwards the memories woven into the etheric body pass out into the universal cosmic ether, and dissolve. And so, for two, three or four days after death, a person experiences this dissolving of his accumulated store of memories. This may be called the laying aside of the etheric body, but it involves an ever-increasing enhancement of the memories; they lose the third dimension and become two-dimensional, entirely picture-like. After the gate of death is passed, the person is faced with the whole tableau of his life, taking its course in vivid pictures for two, three or four days, the time varying with each individual.

But just as a student of botany recognises in a seed the plant that will develop from it, so anyone with Imaginative cognition does not see only at death this passing over of the etheric, of the whole memory system, to the cosmos; he has seen it already in picture form, for as a picture it is always present in human beings. Those who can grasp rightly the interweaving that goes on in the course of three days or more see already, in this incorporation of experiences in the etheric body, a picture of the inward experience that is lived through for three or four days after death. Whereas in earthly existence, before acquiring Imaginative cognition, a man experiences more or less unconsciously this blending of his experiences into the memories held together by the physical body, immediately after death he experiences the reverse process, the unwinding, as it were, of his memories and the passing away of them into the Cosmos. Our treasured thoughts, left behind whenever we fall asleep, unite directly after death with the whole Cosmos. This is what in dying we have to yield up to cosmic existence.

These things must not be grasped only intellectually, but also with heart and soul. For in face of them a man feels that his life is not to be taken egoistically, but that he is placed in the world as a thinking being. He will feel that his thoughts are not something he can preserve, for after his death they will flow out into the Cosmos and will go on working there as active forces. If we have had good thoughts, we surrender them to the Cosmos, and if we have had bad thoughts, we surrender them also. For a man does not exist on earth merely to develop himself as a free being. This he certainly should do, and he can do it precisely if he takes something else into consideration. He is here also as a being on whom the Gods themselves may work, in order to lead the Cosmos on from epoch to epoch. Moreover I would say this : What the Gods are to weave into the Cosmos as thoughts has to be prepared by them through all that can be thought and produced during individual human lives. Here is the nurturing-place where the Gods have to tend the thoughts they need for the continuing evolution of the world—thoughts they then incorporate into the Cosmos as active impulses.

During sleep, a man lives with his Ego and astral organisation outside his physical and etheric bodies. While in this state as a being of soul and spirit, as Ego and astral organisation, he is interwoven with the spiritual forces pervading the whole Cosmos. He is in the world that is, figuratively speaking, outside his skin—the world of which the only impressions he receives in waking life come through his senses. During sleep, therefore, he enters right into the things that in waking life show him only their outer side. But it is only what is experienced by the astral organisation, when outside the physical and etheric bodies, that can be brought back into the thoughts of the etheric body, not what is experienced out there by the Ego. Hence, during the whole of our existence on Earth, the experiences of the Ego in sleep remain subconscious for ordinary consciousness, and even for Imaginative consciousness. They are revealed only to Inspired consciousness, as already described.

So this may be said: In sleep a man gathers up sufficient strength to imprint on the etheric body those experiences that can be put into thoughts. But during his life on Earth he lacks the power to deal with the wishes and desires which during sleep are experienced by the Ego in connection with earthly affairs—for these also are gone over during sleep. In our epoch, therefore, only the part of sleep-life that can be transformed into thoughts, imprinted in thoughts, passes over into the conscious waking life of earthly men; while the sleep-experiences of the Ego lie hidden behind the veil of existence.

Imaginative and Inspired consciousness bring to light here things which can be perfectly well understood by any impartial person with a healthy mind, but in our present civilisation they encounter tremendous prejudice. Even the fact that when the three-dimensional in the physical world is imprinted in the etheric body, it changes from the plastic to a picture form, from three to two dimensions—even to grasp this calls for an unprejudiced approach. Directly we rise to Imagination, we no longer have to do with three dimensions, any more than with four, as a misguided science believes, but with two only. The difficulty of picturing what is then experienced comes from our being accustomed in earthly experience to reckon with three dimensions and to form our concepts accordingly. And so, when we should be finding our way over to two dimensions, we say: "Yes, but two dimensions are included in the three; the two dimensions of a plane can lie in such a way that there might still be a third."

That, however, is not the point. As soon as we enter the

Imaginative world, the third dimension no longer concerns us at all, and the position of a plane is immaterial. On our entering the etheric world of Imagination, the third dimension ceases to have any meaning. Hence—and I add this for mathematicians—all equations for the ether must be transformed so as to correspond with the two-dimensional world.

Now if we would pass on to the world accessible to Inspiration, in which we are as Ego between going to sleep and waking, we come to one dimension only; we then have to do with a one-dimensional world. This transition to a one-dimensional world, taken for granted by the faculty of Inspiration—the faculty, that is, of actually perceiving the spiritual in which we live between going to sleep and waking—this understanding of a world with only one dimension has always been part of Initiation-knowledge.

I have already described how the hidden forces of the Sun—not the forces of the external physical sunlight—are revealed to men of the Jacob Boehme type. These hidden Sun-forces do not spread out three-dimensionally, but are perceived in one dimension only. An older, more instinctive Initiation-knowledge could, and did, come to perceive this through Inspiration, but without a clearly conscious knowledge of what it was. Much that is still handed down in the ancient records of long past epochs of mankind is to be understood only when one knows : This refers to the spiritual world that is one-dimensional, the world we find through Inspiration; as regards our earthly life it refers to the hidden forces of the Sun and Stars. Between going to sleep and waking we do not live in Sun-forces that are outwardly displayed, but in those that are hidden.

These hidden forces of the Sun can, for example, pass through certain kinds of stone which are impenetrable to physically perceptible Sun-forces, and by passing through them become one-dimensional. If anyone has acquired Inspirational vision, then, although he may not perceive the physical light, he can see the hidden Sun-forces penetrating the otherwise opaque stone; thus the stone is permeable for the Sun's hidden forces and also for the forces of Inspiration.

In very ancient periods of human evolution on Earth, such expedients were not needed. But when the old instinctive clairvoyance, which in those days was the basis of Initiation-knowledge, was on the wane, these aids were adopted as a short cut—we might say—to the perception of things no longer perceptible through instinctive Inspiration. People had recourse to such measures in the following way, for example. Imagine a number of stones set up beside one another, with other stones laid across the tops of them. If this is so arranged that on certain occasions the penetrating rays of the Sun fall on the covering stone, then the physical rays of the Sun will be held up by the stone and the hidden rays will pass through.

When anyone trained to it places himself so that he can look into this structure from the side, he will see the spiritual, one-dimensional rays of the Sun shining through and vanishing into the earth. If, when all this was no longer perceived through instinctive clairvoyant powers, a short cut of that kind were taken, it enabled anyone looking from the side into the shadow-zone to perceive the world of spiritual Sun-rays which we experience every night during sleep. Hence in such contrivances, to be met with in this very district, we can see by what means, during a long transitional period, certain wise leaders of mankind tried to penetrate to the hidden forces of the Sun, which a man such as Jacob Boehme could do instinctively through simply beholding earthly things.

Although such collections of stones can be seen to-day in appropriate places, their real significance can be brought out only through what Spiritual Science reveals. Otherwise people are left with a superficial explanation which misses the real point.

Such stones can of course be distributed in the circle so as to show how the spiritual rays of the Sun differ according to particular constellations of the stars.

I have been trying to make clear to you the world in which our Ego lives during sleep. This world is not held together by the inherent forces of the physical and etheric bodies. These

bodies, however, are alone responsible for the clear consciousness of earthly man; they are the source of the judgments we
form, in accordance with our feelings and our will, on our
own actions, our inward experiences and thoughts. Hence,
when we are awake, we judge our external life according to
the thoughts we have been able to imprint in our physical and
etheric bodies. But it is not only a human being himself who
has something to say about his experiences; his experiences and
actions are the concern of the whole spiritual Cosmos. The
Cosmos judges whether an action, a thought or feeling is to
be declared good or bad. Between waking and sleeping we are
left to form our own opinions about ourselves. As I have
sufficiently shown during these lectures, the spiritual content
of the Cosmos takes the moral as its natural law, and what the
Cosmos has to say about our true nature and our actions is
experienced by the Ego during sleep. Inspired cognition shows
how the Ego, even during the shortest sleep, experiences over
again everything the individual has gone through from his last
moment of waking until his present sleep—however long or
short this period may be. So a man, in the successive states of
waking, sleeping, waking, sleeping, experiences again in sleep
whatever he went through during his last waking time, especially where his own activities were concerned.

As far as this is the experience of the Ego, it remains outside ordinary consciousness, but Inspiration can call it up.
Then the particular nature of the experience is disclosed, and
we find it is gone through in reverse order to our
experience by day. Whereas by day you go through your experiences—leaving short sleeps aside—from morning to evening, during the night, in sleep, you live through these experiences backwards—from evening to morning. This is in order
that we may experience whatever the spiritual Cosmos has
to say about the way we have lived through the day.

During earthly life, however, a man cannot normally call
this experience up into consciousness. Yet he must become
conscious of it, or his human existence would fall out of connection with cosmic existence. Inspired cognition shows that
as soon as a man after death has watched his life-tableau,

which, as I have said, lasts two, three, or four days, and as soon as his memories have dissolved into the Cosmos, spreading themselves out there—after this experience, often referred to as the freeing of the etheric body—a time comes when the man is able to look back on his earthly life again, but in a different way.

If we look at those few days after death, we come to a mighty panorama of our life, but at first it embraces daytime experiences alone. In reality, however, a man goes through not only his waking experiences but also those he has had during sleep. When in earthly life you look back on your ordinary memories, you always leave out your periods of sleep, as if your only experiences had been those lived through by day. And so it goes on right back to the time after birth when your memories cease.

In fact it is like this with the panorama that appears during those two or three days after death. Then, later, comes a period when soul and spirit have gained sufficient strength to experience in the spiritual world all that could manifest only unconsciously, in picture form, while we were asleep at night during our life on Earth. It now comes before us as experience. A man then passes through a period—lasting about one-third of his life on Earth, approximately the time normally spent in sleep—when he experiences his nights again, but in a backward direction. So he lives through his last night first, then the night before, and so on right back to the time of his birth and conception.

From other points of view I have described this going back through a quite different world after death in my book, *Theosophy*, when I was speaking of man, as a being of soul and spirit, passing through the soul-world.

Now when after death a man has gone thus through the soul-world, taking about seven years for it if he has lived twenty-one years, or, if he has lived to sixty, perhaps twenty years—always the length of time he has slept in earthly life— he has then to experience the total effect he has had upon Earth-existence—an existence created by the Gods in order to carry the world, with the help of the human race, a little further on its progress. Up to the end of this backward survey of his nights after death, a man has been gaining knowledge of what he has himself become, of his significance for the Cosmos. He now has to experience how the Earth itself has been affected by his life. This takes a long time—half the time, indeed, between earthly death and a new earthly life. To-morrow we shall have to speak of this in greater detail.

After going backwards through our nights, we come to our birth; and having arrived there, after this backward journey through the soul-world, we have to find the way back to our previous earthly life. This enables a man to bring over with him that previous life for the shaping of his next life on Earth.

Here we enter the realm of the old Initiation-knowledge (which must be renewed to-day in a way suited to men's present faculties.) The old Initiation-knowledge led people over to religious experience. For Initiation-knowledge is always true knowledge, but of a kind that leads out from the world of the senses into the spiritual, so that the human will is stirred to take a religious form. At the stage of Initiation which leads to the Intuitive-knowledge already described, it has always been recognised as of the utmost importance that when a man goes back to his previous life on Earth, he should meet on the way a being who can become his guide after death.

In a certain region of the Earth a man would say to himself : In my earthly life I must absorb the teaching of the last Bodhisattva to appear on earth. The man may have lived three hundred years after the appearance of this Bodhisattva. But when after death he went back to his previous life on Earth, he arrived at the time when the last Bodhisattva was living on Earth. In the old Initiation-knowledge, this meeting with the last Bodhisattva to appear on the Earth was regarded as enabling the man to make a real contact with his own previous earthly life—which means finding the necessary strength for eternal life, for this can be found only when real contact with the previous earthly life is achieved.

Any possibility of this meeting with the Bodhisattvas, who descend to Earth from certain spiritual regions, ceased at a definite time in human evolution, in world-evolution. And to-day a man would have been unable, when after death he had gone back to his last birth and conception, to go further and make contact with his previous earthly lives. The way to this could be found by a man during the first millennia of earthly evolution before the Mystery of Golgotha, when, in going back, he came to the time of the last Bodhisattva. To-day, however, he will find the way only if he makes the journey under the leadership of that Being who united Himself with the Earth through the Mystery of Golgotha; if, in other words, he enters into such a relation with the Mystery of Golgotha that Christ can become his guide. For the Christ gathers into Himself all those powers of leadership for life between death and rebirth which used to belong to the Bodhisattvas who appeared on Earth.

Thus the event of the Mystery of Golgotha, with its particular bearing on our experience between death and rebirth, is one of the most important facts in the whole evolution of the Earth. If anyone wishes to learn about the spiritual evolution of the Earth and the place it takes in the spiritual evolution of the Cosmos, and if moreover he wishes to understand what a man goes through in connection with this spiritual evolution of Earth and Cosmos during his life between death and a new birth, then he must give the Mystery of Golgotha its right place in the whole evolution of the world. For people to-day, therefore, a way must be found that will lead attention over from the evolution of man to the evolution of the world, so that the Mystery of Golgotha is seen in all its fundamental significance for the course of events in the evolution of the Earth and in the evolution of man within the earthly.

With these matters, as far as modern Initiation-knowledge can reveal them—matters relating to the later experiences of human beings after death, when they have gone back in memory through their night-experiences—we will deal further to-morrow, in connection with the evolution of the world.

IX

Experiences between Death and Rebirth

I began my lecture yesterday with a brief outline of a man's experiences in sleep, and of how in a certain sense they presage his experiences after death. These sleep-experiences lie beyond the so-called threshold which, in course of our days here, has often been mentioned. The experiences I am now going to describe are gone through by all human beings when asleep, though they do not rise up into ordinary consciousness in life on Earth, but are accessible only to Imagination, Inspiration and Intuition. Because they do not enter consciousness, we should not believe they do not exist; they do exist, and we go through them. If I am allowed a simile—it is as though a man were led through a room blindfold. He does not see anything, but he has to exert himself to walk, and he can have some experience of many things in the room, although he cannot see them. What I am going to describe concerning the time betwen going to sleep and waking is plunged, as it were, in darkness, since the consciousness is blind to it, but it is positively lived through by human beings, and the effects of all we experience in sleep enter our waking life. Thus we understand rightly what anyone goes through, from the time of waking until going to sleep, only when we look upon it as combining the after-effect of his last sleep with whatever he does through his physical and etheric bodies during the day.

Now when a man goes to sleep, at first an indefinite feeling of anxiety comes over him. In ordinary life on Earth this anxiety does not rise into consciousness, does not actually manifest; but it is there as a process in the man's astral body and Ego, and he carries over its results into his waking state during the next day. If this anxiety were not carried over, were not to work in waking life as a force in physical body and etheric body, the man would be unable to hold together his physical constitution so that, for example, it may secrete salts and similar substances in the right way. This secretion, necessary for the organism, is throughout an effect of subconscious anxiety during the life of sleep. First of all in sleep, therefore, we enter what I might call a sphere of anxiety.

Then a condition arises in the soul like a continuous swinging to and fro, from a state of inner tranquility to one of uneasiness—such a movement to and fro that, if the man were conscious of it, he might believe he was alternately beginning to faint and then recovering. Thus the anxiety sets going a constant alternation between self-control and the losing of it.

Thirdly comes a feeling of standing on the brink of an abyss with the ground giving way under one's feet, so that at any moment one might fall into the depths.

You see that at this moment when a man is falling asleep, conditions in the Cosmos are already beginning to rise from the physical to the moral. For the second state we enter on going to sleep can be properly judged only when we recognise that moral laws in the Cosmos have the validity of natural laws on Earth—only, that is, when we feel their reality with the same certainty we have in speaking of a stone falling to the ground, or of an engine driven by its steam. Nevertheless, in earthly life, because a man's strength is still limited, he is for the present protected by the kindly guidance of the world from experiencing consciously all that he goes through unconsciously every night.

The ordering of the Cosmos is such that even the things which shine out in the greatest beauty, the most lofty splendour, must have their roots in sorrow, suffering and renunciation. In the background of every beautiful appearance are pain and self-denial. In the universe this is just as inevitable as that the angles of a triangle should add up to 180 degrees. It is mere foolishness to ask why the Gods have not so organised the Cosmos that it would give men pleasure only. They bring about necessities. This was indeed divined in the Egyptian Mysteries, for example. They called the conscious perception of what occurs in sleep—the anxiety, the swinging to and fro between keeping hold of oneself and become powerless, and the standing on the brink of an abyss—the world of the three iron necessities.

These experiences during sleep produce in the man, again unconsciously, a profound yearning towards the divine which he then feels to be filling, penetrating, permeating, the whole Cosmos. For him, then, the Cosmos resolves itself into a kind of hovering, weaving, ever-moving cloud-formation, in which one is living, able at every moment to feel oneself alive, but at the same time realising that at any moment one could be submerged in all this weaving and living. A man feels himself interwoven with the weaving, surging movement of the divine throughout the world. And in the pantheistic feeling for God which comes to every healthy human being during waking life, there is the aftermath, the consequence, of the pantheistic feeling for God which is experienced unconsciously during sleep. A man then feels his soul to be filled with an inner unconscious conviction, born, one might say, out of anxiety and powerlessness; and filled also with something like an inner force of gravity in place of the ordinary gravity of the physical world.

The Rosicrucian mystery-teachings gave expression to what comes over a man when he sinks into the realm of the three iron necessities. The experience that would come to the pupils immediately after going to sleep was explained. They were told: Your daytime experiences sink into moving, floating cloud-formations, but these reveal themselves as having the nature of beings. You yourself are interwoven with these clouds, and you hover in anxiety and powerlessness on the edge of an abyss. But you have already discovered what then should be brought to your consciousness in three words— words which should pervade your whole soul: *Ex Deo nascimur.* This *Ex Deo nascimur,* so vague for ordinary consciousness, but raised into consciousness for students of the new Mysteries, is what a man first experiences on entering the state of sleep.

Later in these lectures we shall see how this *Ex Deo nasci-mur* plays an historic part also in the world-evolution of mankind. What I am now describing is the part it plays during earthly existence in the life of each single man, personally, individually.

If the man continues to sleep, the next stage is that the ordinary view of the Cosmos, as seen from the Earth, ceases. Whereas at night the Earth the glittering, shining stars are there for him, together with the Moon, and by day the Sun playing upon his senses, at a certain moment during sleep he sees how this whole starry world vanishes. The stars cease as physical entities, but in the places where they appeared physically to the senses there come forth from their rays—which have vanished—the genii, the spirits, the gods, of the stars. For conscious Inspiration the Cosmos changes into a speaking universe, declaring itself through the music of the spheres and the cosmic word. The Cosmos is then made up of living spiritual beings, in place of the Cosmos visible to the senses from the Earth.

This is experienced in such a way that, if a man became conscious of it, he would feel as if the whole spiritual Cosmos, from every side, was pronouncing judgment on what he has made of himself as a human being through all his deeds, both good and evil. He would feel that in his human worth he was bound up with the Cosmos.

What comes to him first of all, however—and if he could experience it consciously, as Inspiration does, he would notice this—is bewildering, and he has need of a guide. In the present period of human evolution this guide appears if, during life on Earth, a man has woven in his soul and heart a thread uniting him with the Mystery of Golgotha; if, that is, he has created a bond with the Christ, who, as Jesus, went through the Mystery of Golgotha. The feeling that immediately lays hold of a man at the present time—we will speak tomorrow of other epochs—is that, in the sphere he now enters, his bewildered soul would surely disintegrate if the Being who has come to be the very life of his conceptions and feelings, and of the impulses of his heart—if the Christ were not to be his Guide.

The approach of the Christ as Guide—who in this sphere

must be conceived of as connected with the life of the Sun, just as the man is connected with earthly life—is felt again in the same way that it was when a medieval Mystery School brought it before the souls of the pupils with the words: *In Christo morimur*. For the feeling is that the soul must perish should it not die in Christ, thereby dying into cosmic life.

In this way a man lives through the experiences of sleep. After perceiving the stars of the Cosmos in their essential being, and because he cannot attain to conscious wakefulness in this sphere, a longing comes over him to return to the sphere where he is conscious. That is why we wake; it is the force by which we are awakened. We develop an unconscious feeling that, because of what we have absorbed from the real being of the stars, from the star Gods, we shall not be spiritually empty when we wake; for we bring down with us, into the daily life of the body, the spirit dwelling in our soul.

The pupils in the medieval Mystery Centres were made aware of this feeling, the third in the series of nightly, personal experiences of human beings on Earth, by a third saying: *Per spiritum sanctum reviviscimus*. This threefold experience of the spiritual world lying beyond the Guardian of the Threshold—who is ignored only by men of the present epoch —is thus perceptible in three stages, and at the same time they imprint on the human soul what can truly be called the Trinity—the Trinity which permeates spiritual life, weaving and living throughout it.

What I have been describing here is experienced by a man every night in a picture, and into this picture are woven his daytime experiences, going backwards in time. Just as we find our earthly experiences interwoven with those of natural processes during waking life, so during the night we experience this backward repetition interwoven with memories of the starry world. But all this is at first a picture.

This can be realised only when a man has gone through the gate of death. Here on Earth it is a picture experienced backwards. It becomes real only when, after three or four days, we have completed the panoramic survey of our memories described yesterday, and we enter the spiritual world no longer in terms of pictures, as we do every night, but in reality.

If anyone wishes to bring before his soul with a right understanding the experiences that are gone through consciously after the gate of death is passed, the following must be borne in mind. The Gods, the spiritual Beings we meet from the metamorphosed stars, take a different cosmic direction in their lives from that followed by human beings in earthly existence. Here we touch on a very important truth about the spiritual worlds, though it is not generally recognised when the spiritual worlds are spoken of theoretically and with little perception. When we are conscious as earthly men in earthly existence, we have a physical body and an etheric body so organised that a later experience always follows an earlier one and we find ourselves carried along in a particular stream of time. It is characteristic of our physical and etheric bodies to take this direction in the Cosmos. In so far as we are human beings, we experience everything in this sequence.

Those beings whom we met on rising to life between death and rebirth—when we discover the reality behind the pictures of our sleep-experience—move and come towards us always from the opposite direction. So that, in accordance with what in earthly life is called time, we must say : The Gods have spiritual bodies—one could equally well say, bodies of light —with which they move from the most distant future towards the past.

During the time between death and rebirth our bodies are of this same nature; we acquire them just as here on Earth we acquire the physical substance of our physical body. Divine bodies clothe us, and with them we draw round us what in my book *Theosophy* I have called Spirit-Man and Life-Spirit. By so doing we find our direction reversed, and so we live through our life backwards until we reach our birth and conception. In life on Earth we start from birth or conception, and—if we think of a circle—during existence on Earth we complete the top half. When that existence is over, we

return through the lower half of the circle to our birth and conception. Just as on leaving our home we might walk in a
certain direction and return, completing a circle in space, so
—since in the world we enter after death there is no space—
we have now to complete a circle in *time*. In time, it is a
going out and coming back. Between birth and death we
go out and then, having had this experience, we go backwards through the experiences of our nights as spiritual
realities, until we return to the point of time at which we
started.

In this materialistically thinking age little is said about such
circles of life, and we have to go back in human evolution on
Earth if we are to find words to express what really happens.
If we turn to the old Oriental wisdom, with its less conscious
insight into things than we have to-day, and its dreamlike
clairvoyance, we find there a wonderful expression, evidently
derived from an insight we can recover if we cross the threshold with real understanding, and pass the Guardian consciously when entering the spiritual world.

When the spiritual world is described in theories built up
at any rate half-intellectually, it is not far removed from a
materialistic picture of the Cosmos. It shows a human being
as beginning his life at birth, then becoming a child and later
a youth or young girl, growing older and approaching death
—and then on and on in a straight line which naturally is
never brought to an end. Anyone with knowledge of Initiation
knows how nonsensical it is to talk of an end. This road has
no ending : it turns back on itself. And the wonderful expression used by the old Oriental Initiates to describe this
fact is "the wheel of births".

There is much talk of this "wheel of births", but little of
it nowadays points to the truth. In fact we have accomplished
the first revolution of this wheel at the end of our journey
around the stars, which takes about one-third of our whole
earthly life—the time, that is, we spend in sleep on Earth.
We have then completed the first revolution, and in the
life between death and rebirth we can await further revolu-
tions of the wheel.

That is how it is when, with knowledge awakened through Imagination, Inspiration and Intuition, we make our way into the worlds lying behind the veil of the sense-world. These are worlds that once, in a remote period of evolution, were open to man as a heritage from a past age, when he associated with divine-spiritual Beings in the way described. It is only when some insight into the spiritual worlds takes us back to ancient times, when people knew about these worlds, that it becomes possible to understand all that has come down to us from the old wisdom. And then we are filled with wonder at this primeval wisdom of mankind. So that anyone who has received Initiation at the present time can do no other than look up to those ancient days of man's earthly existence with admiration, with reverence.

Something else can be seen from this—that only through the Spiritual Science of to-day can we arrive again at the true form in which things were perceived of old. People who want to shut out modern Spiritual Science have no means of understanding the language spoken by those who possessed the primeval wisdom of mankind; hence they are fundamentally unable to picture things historically. Those who know nothing of the spiritual world are often quite naive in the way they expound and interpret the old records of primeval peoples. So, in documents which perhaps contain primeval wisdom now obscured, we find ringing out such wonderful words as "the wheel of births". These words must be understood by rediscovering the reality to which they allude. People who want to give a picture of the true history of mankind on Earth must therefore not shrink from first learning to know the meaning of the language used in those far-off days.

I might very well have begun by picturing the historical evolution of mankind in the terms used in the ancient records; but then you would not have heard words used merely as words, as they so often are in the world to-day. Hence, if one is to give a true picture of that part of the world of reality lived through by a man during his historical period, one has to start by describing his relation to the spiritual worlds. For only in this way are we enabled to find our way about in the language used, and in all that was done in those ancient times to maintain a connection with the spiritual worlds.

Yesterday I described how the Druid priests set up stones and screened them in such a way that, by gazing into the shadow thrown within this structure and looking through the stones, they could gain information concerning the will of the spiritual worlds which impressed itself into the physical. But something else also was connected with this. In the spiritual world there is not only a going away, but also always a coming back. Just as there are forces of time which carry us forward through physical existence on Earth, and after death draw us backwards again, so, in the structures set up by the Druids, there are forces descending from above and also forces ascending from below. Hence in these structures the Druid priests watched both a downward and an upward stream. When their structures were set up on appropriate sites, the priests could perceive not only the will of divine Spirits coming down from the Cosmos but—because in the upward stream the one-dimensional prevailed—they could perceive the good or bad elements which belonged to members of their community and flowed out from them into the Cosmos. Thus these stones served as an observatory for the Druid priests, enabling them to see how the souls of their people stood in relation to the Cosmos.*

All these secrets, all these mysteries, are connected with things that have remained from ancient times, and exist now in so decadent a form. They can be understood only when through the power of individual Imagination, Inspiration and Intuition, the world of the Spirit is raised once more out of its hidden existence and brought into consciousness.

These circular movements—which are of course meant

---

* See *Man in the Past, the Present and the Future* by Rudolf Steiner, Rudolf Steiner Press, London 1966 (Ed.).

metaphorically, since one is moving in the one-dimensional realm—are gone through repeatedly during a man's life between death and a new birth. And as with this revolution—going out from birth to death and returning from death to birth—so do others take their course in the whole of a man's life between death and rebirth, but in such a way that there is always a change of level between the experience of the going out and the experience of returning. In the first round of the wheel of birth, the distinction lies in our experiencing the out-going half up to death, and the return half—which lasts, when measured by earthly time, for a third of our life on Earth—immediately after physical death. Then the first round has been completed. Others follow, and we go on making such rounds until we come to a very definite place from which we can journey back in the way I shall be picturing to-morrow. We continue to complete these rounds of the wheel until we reach the point, in our life as a whole, which indicates the death we experienced in our last incarnation.

Thus in circles—though our first experience after death is a looking backwards, a living backwards—we live through what we underwent between our last death and last birth into Earth-existence. Each of these circular journeys corresponds in its outgoing to a cosmic life of sleep. If one were to describe further these circles, one would say that the outgoing always corresponds with a life after death, in that a man with his whole being goes out more into the cosmic world and is conscious of living within it—of becoming one with it.

When a man comes back into himself from the cosmic world, this return corresponds with his working on what he has experienced there, and now realises to be united with himself. As here on Earth we must have alternate sleeping and waking for a healthy life, between death and a new birth we have always to experience a flowing out into the Cosmos, when we feel ourselves to be as great and all-embracing as the Cosmos itself, and perceive the creations and deeds of the Cosmos as our own. We identify ourselves with the whole Universe so entirely that we say : That which you beheld with

your physical eyes as an Earth-dweller; that which looked
down on you in its physical reflection as the Cosmos of stars—
in this you are now living. It is not, however, as physical stars
but as divine-spiritual Beings that they are now uniting their
existence with yours. You have, as it were, dissolved into the
life of the Cosmos, and the divine-spiritual Beings of the
Cosmos are living within you. You have identified yourself
with them. That is one part of the experience we pass through
between death and a new birth—whether you call it cosmic
night or cosmic day. The terms used on Earth are naturally a
matter of indifference to the Gods living in the spiritual world.
In order to bring home to ourselves what we experience out
there, we have to use earthly forms of speech, but they must
be such as will correspond with the reality.

The times in which we grow together with the Cosmos,
identify ourselves with the whole Cosmos, are followed by other
times when we draw back, as it were, into a single point
within ourselves—when everything we first experienced as
being poured out into the whole Cosmos is now felt as a cosmic memory, inwardly united with ourselves. We feel the
wheel of births as though perpetually turning, carrying us out
into the Cosmos and back into ourselves, there to experience in
miniature what we have lived through out there. Then we go
out again, and return again, following a spiral path. The wheel
of births can indeed be described as a spiral movement, perpetually turning in on itself. In this way, between death and a
new birth, we progress through an alternation of self-experi-
ence and self-surrender. To say this, however, takes us only as
far as if we were to describe events on Earth in the course of
the twenty-four hours by saying: Human beings sleep and
wake. We have merely gone that far with such a description
of a man's experience between death and a new birth in the
spiritual world. For the outgoing surrender and the drawing
back again of the self in the spiritual world are similar to
waking and sleeping in earthly life. And as in earthly life
only those events a man has lived through find a place, so in
the completion of these wheels of births and deaths the

spiritual events involved are those a man has actually experienced between death and rebirth. In order to grasp these
events we must form a sound conception of how matters really
stand for a man in earthly life.

Strictly speaking, a man is awake only in his conceptual
world and in a closely connected part of his world of feeling.
When he intends to do anything, if only to pick up a pencil,
his intention lives in a concept and shoots down into the will,
which then makes a demand on the muscles, until the further
concept of having grasped the pencil comes to him. All this
activity, expressing his will and desire, remains shrouded in
darkness for his earthly consciousness; it resembles his life of
sleep. Only in our concepts and in part of our feeling-life
are we normally awake. In the other part of our feeling, the
part that approves or disapproves the actions of the will, and
in the will itself, we are asleep.

Now we do not take our thoughts with us after death. We
take them into that life after death as little as we take them
with us at night. In the world between death and a new birth
we have to form our own thoughts in keeping with that world.
We do, however, take with us that which lies in our subconscious—our will and the part of our feeling connected
with it. It is precisely with everything of which we are unconscious in earthly life, with all that lives in our impulses and
desires, and in our will influenced by the senses, and with all
that lives spiritually in our will—it is with all this that we go
through the time between death and rebirth, making conscious
our cosmic thoughts about our unconscious experiences on
Earth.

If we wish to understand the times lived through immediately beyond the gate of death, we must be clear that the
experiences which come to the soul from the physical body
take on another aspect directly we no longer possess a physical body. It is not your physical body, with its chemical substances, that experiences hunger and thirst; these are experiences of the soul. But it is through the physical body that all
such cravings are satisfied here on Earth. Hunger lives in the
soul, and in earthly life hunger is satisfied through the body;

through the body thirst is quenched, although thirst, too, lives
in the soul. When you have passed the gate of death you
no longer have a physical body, but you still have thirst and
hunger. You carry them through the gate of death, and for a
third of the length of your life on Earth, while you are going
backwards through your nights, you have time to disaccus-
tom yourself from thirst, hunger, and all other desires experienced only through the body. Herein consists the inner experience after death of this third of your life on Earth:
everything that can be gratified only through the body—or at
any rate only in earthly life—is purged from the soul, and the
soul is freed from these desires. We shall see later what lies
further on.

I have now given you a description of part of a man's experience after he passes through the gate of death—a description based on what we have gone into to-day. To-morrow we
will look further into the life between death and rebirth, in its
connection with the whole earthly evolution of mankind. We
must, however, be clear about the scope of the events which
enter into earthly life. A great deal that can now be investi-
gated only through Imagination, Inspiration and Intuition
was at one time open to people through a kind of instinctive
vision. The night was not such a closed book for them. Their
waking life took a more dreamlike course, and in its dream-
pictures revealed more of the spiritual world.

I should like now to draw attention to something you will
see more clearly during the next few days. We are living in an
age when human beings are exposed in the highest degree to
the danger of losing all connection with the spiritual world.
And perhaps, as we are so close here to centres reminiscent
of the old European Druids, it will be appropriate to mention
certain symptoms, which, though not harmful in themselves,
show not only what is taking place on Earth but also what is
happening spiritually behind the scenes of existence.

Now consider medieval man, including his shadow-side;
consider the so-called Dark Ages; compare all this with mankind to-day. I will take only two symptoms which can show
us how, from the spiritual standpoint, we should look upon

the world. Turn to a medieval book. Every single letter is as though painted in. We seem actually to see how the eye rested on those characters. The writer's whole mood of soul, when it rested upon the written letters in those days, was attuned to enter deeply into whatever could come to him as revelations of the spiritual worlds.

And now consider a great deal of handwriting to-day—it is hardly legible! The letters cannot give one anything like the pleasure one has from a painting; they are thrown on the paper as though with a mechanical movement of the hand—or so it appears very often. Moreover the time is already beginning when there will no longer be any writing by hand—nothing but typewriting—and we shall no longer experience any connection with the words on the paper. This, and the motorcar, are the two symptoms which show what is going on behind the scenes of existence, and how human beings are driven away more and more from the spiritual world.

Do not think I want to come before you as a typical reactionary who would like to put a stop to cars and typewriters, or even to this terrible handwriting. Anyone who realises how the world is going knows very well that such things have to be; they are justified. Hence there is no question of abolishing them; I am saying only that in dealing with them we should be on our guard. These things have to come and must be accepted in the same way that we accept night and day, although enthusiasm for them may be found chiefly among people who are strongly inclined to materialism. All these developments, however, the illegible handwriting, the distressing noise of typewriters, and the quite horrible rushing of motorcars—all this has to be faced in order that men should rightly develop a vigorous approach to spiritual knowledge, spiritual feeling, and spiritual will. There is no question of fighting against the material, but of getting to know its reality and necessity; and also of seeing how essential it is that strength of spirit should be brought to bear against the crushing weight of physical existence. Then, through a swing of the pendulum between cars and typewriters and Imaginations and insight into the spiritual world—the fruits of spiritual-scientific work—the healthy development of mankind can be furthered, which otherwise can only be prejudiced.

This has to be said particularly in Penmaenmawr, for here, on the one hand, we perceive how the Imaginations from the old days of the Druids remain, as I have already described; while on the other hand we discover how forcibly these Imaginations are destroyed by the rushing of motorcars through the atmosphere.

X

Man's Life after Death in the Spiritual Cosmos

If we wish to bring before our souls the nature of our experiences between death and rebirth, we must above all grasp the great difference between them and those of earthly life. Here on Earth we carry out whatever we do in such a way that once done, it separates from us—it no longer belongs to us. For example, we manufacture various things and they become detached from us. Most people get free of them by selling them. Hence we find that anything a man makes on Earth, as the outcome of his will, goes out into the world in such a way that he feels relatively—I say expressly, relatively—little connection with it. And the thoughts out of which he creates something on Earth slip back within him, into his inner being, where they either remain merely passive or become memories, habits, aptitudes.

It is different between death and a new birth. There, everything a man achieves flows back to him, in a certain sense.

Now we must remember that here on Earth we carry out the impulses of our will on things belonging to the kingdoms of nature—on the minerals, plants and animals. We more or less mould them, move them around, and even set other people into motion.

In the spiritual world, between death and rebirth, we are among purely spiritual Beings, partly with those whose whole existence has been in the spiritual world, who have never been incorporated in earthly substance. Among such Beings belong the higher Hierarchies—the Angels, the Exusiai, the Seraphim and Cherubim. Other names may be preferred; but here, too, there is no need to quarrel over terminology. These particular names are old and venerable; they may well be used now for what we are rediscovering in spiritual realms.

Between his death and rebirth, accordingly, a man dwells

partly among such Beings, and partly with the souls of men who have cast off their earthly bodies and taken on spiritual ones; or with those souls who are awaiting their coming re-descent to Earth. This co-existence, it is true, depends somewhat on whether we are connected with such souls, whether we have formed a bond with them in earthly life. For those persons with whom we have not been in close contact on Earth have little to do with us in the spiritual world. I shall have more to say about this.

Then, too, a man stands in relation to other beings who have never been so directly incorporated in earthly life as he was himself, for they are at a lower stage and not ready to take on human form. These are the elemental beings who live in the kingdoms of nature, in the plant kingdom, in the kingdom of the rocks, of the minerals, as well as in that of the animals. Thus, between death and rebirth, a man grows together with the whole spirit-populated world.

I must add that these beings are perceptible to Inspired, Intuitive and Imaginative consciousness, for with these forms of consciousness one can see into the world where we live between death and a new birth.

Because a man lives then in a quite different way, his whole mood and condition are changed. When here on Earth, for example—I am coming back to this same important theme—we make a machine, our action, the handling and fitting together of the parts, flow from our will and our thoughts. But all this becomes detached from us. When between death and a new birth we are in the spiritual world—where as souls we are continually active, always doing something—there shines out from our actions something we recognise as thoughts living in light. Here on Earth a thought stays with us; there, it shines out in everything we do, gleaming as a being of light. So that in the spiritual world we can never do anything without a thought springing from it. This thought is not like the thought of an earthly human being which he can often conceal, however harmful it may be, for it is a personal, individual thought. But in the life between death and rebirth the thought which springs out of things is a cosmic thought, expressing the response of the whole spiritual cosmic world to what we are doing.

Now picture this to yourselves vividly. In the life between death and a new birth a man is active. Through his activity, every action by the soul, every grasping, one might say every touch, immediately changes into a cosmic thought, so that in doing anything we imprint it on the spiritual world. Then on all sides an answer rings back from the Cosmos; out of what we do there flashes up what the Cosmos says of it, and this cosmic verdict is final. But that is not all. In this flashing up of the cosmic world of thought, something else glimmers—other thoughts which we cannot say originate in the Cosmos. Thus we find the brilliantly flashing thoughts permeated by all sorts of dark thoughts, glimmering out of our surroundings.

While the brightly gleaming thoughts from the Cosmos fill us with a profound feeling of pleasure, the glimmering ones—very often, though not always—carry something extraordinarily disquieting; for they are thoughts still working on from our life on Earth. If we have cultivated good thoughts during earthly life, they glimmer out, after death, from the radiant cosmic environment. If we have cherished bad thoughts, evil thoughts, they may be said to glimmer out towards us from the shining thoughts of the cosmic verdict.

In this way we behold both what the Cosmos is saying to us and what we ourselves have brought with us to the Cosmos. This is not a world that detaches itself from a person; it remains intimately bound up with him. After death he bears within him his cosmic existence, and, as a memory, his last existence on Earth. His next task is to lay aside this earthly life and to accustom himself to a different way of living, so that he may become a cosmic being in the true sense. As long as we are in that region of spiritual experience which in my book, *Theosophy*, I called the soul-world, we are pre-occupied with this aftermath of glimmering earthly thoughts, earthly ways of life, earthly aptitudes. Because of this we make what we feel could be beautiful cosmic forms into grotesque ones, and so, under the guidance of these distorted cosmic forms during our passage through the soul-world, we wander on through the

Cosmos until we are freed from everything binding us to the Earth. Then we can find our way into the realm called spirit-land in my book, *Theosophy*. We have then left behind the state of soul habitual to us in physical life on Earth, and we are able to act in perfect accordance with the admonitions of those spiritual Beings whose realm we have to enter as the only one where it is possible for us to be.

You will see that a man does not take with him into the world after death anything that lives in his physical and etheric bodies. That is thrown off and sinks away into the Cosmos. He takes with him only what as Ego and astral body he has experienced within his physical and etheric bodies.

Something of outstanding significance and importance follows from this. While a man is going about on Earth, he regards his physical body and his etheric body—of which he knows little, but at least he feels it in his powers of growth, and so on—as his own body, but he has no right to do so. Only his Ego and his astral body are *his*. Everything present in his physical body and etheric body—even while he is on Earth—is the property of the divine-spiritual Beings who live and weave within them, and continue their work while the man is absent in sleep. It would go badly with anyone if he had to care for his own etheric and physical bodies in continual wakefulness between birth and death. Time and time again he is obliged to hand over his physical and etheric bodies to the Gods—especially during childhood, for then sleep is the most important thing of all. Later in life sleep works only as a corrective; the really fructifying sleep is the sleep that comes to a child in the first years of its life. Thus the human being has continually to be yielding up both physical and etheric bodies to the care of the Gods.

In past ages of human evolution this was so clearly perceived that the body was called the temple of the Gods, for so was its wonderful structure experienced. And in all architectural work—this can best be seen in oriental buildings, but also in those of Egypt and of Greece—the laws of the physical body and the etheric body were followed. In the very way the Cherubim are set on the temples of the East, in the attitude of a sphinx, or in the placing of pillars—in all this the work of divine-spiritual Beings in the human physical and etheric bodies has been made to live again. In the course of evolution, consciousness of this has been lost; and to-day we refer to the physical body as our own—with no notion of how unjustified this is—whereas as an earthly creation it belongs in reality to the Gods. Hence, when anyone to-day talks of "my body", when he speaks of the healthy functioning of his body as due to himself, it is just an instance of the prodigious arrogance of modern man—a subconscious pride, certainly, expressed with no awareness of it, but none the less deplorable. It shows how in speaking of their bodies as their own, people are really laying claim to the property of the Gods, and this pride is embodied in their very speech.

To all these things attention must be drawn anew by Spiritual Science; it must show how a moral element is already mixed into our ordinary naturalistic life—and truly, as we have seen in the case just referred to, it can take a by no means healthy form. These matters show how, through genuine spiritual knowledge, our whole feeling life can be so transformed that, if Spiritual Science has been really understood, even ways of speaking can become different from the way in which people like to talk under the influence of purely materialistic thinking.

In order to understand the further experience we have between death and rebirth, we must be able to recall what was said yesterday—that, on growing accustomed to the spiritual world, a man loses the physical aspect of the stars and in its stead there arises the spiritual counterpart of the brilliance of their rays which meet the eye physically. Just as the Earth is the dwelling-place of men who, with their Ego and astral body, live upon it as spiritual beings, so certain spiritual Beings dwell in every single star. And during his physical life a man is connected also with elemental beings dwelling in the kingdoms of the minerals, plants and animals. He is also connected through his ordinary bodily life with other human souls. Then, between death and a new birth, he is in connection with the dwellers on other stars, and his life is actually spent in experiencing the world of the stars through its spiritual counterpart, through life in common with the other divine-spiritual Beings dwelling there.

We have already seen how, immediately after earthly life, we pass through existence in the soul-world, and how it is essentially a living backwards through all that we have slept through in unconscious imagery during our nights on Earth. One-third of the duration of a man's earthly life is thus spent in weaning himself from that which his glimmering thoughts carry into the thoughts of the Cosmos. Anyone who has lived to the age of sixty, say, on Earth, will therefore go through the soul-world in twenty years, while he is working his way out of everything connecting him with physical existence. Inwardly, during this time after death, he experiences his coming into relation with the world of the stars, and especially with the Moon. Yesterday I spoke of a man describing a circle, as it were, completing the first half between birth and death, and the return half in a third of that time. I would now add that he feels this circling to take place round the Moon-existence and the spirits belonging to it. As I pointed out yesterday, he is not conscious of returning to his birth, and so his movement is not actually a circle but a spiral, a progressive spiral.

The reason why we do not simply circle round the Moon, but move on to approach another state of existence, is partly the onward driving force of the Mercury beings. These beings are rather stronger than those of Venus. Existence is urged forward by the Mercury beings, whereas through the Venus beings it is brought to a stop, as though completed. Hence the essential course of a man's passage through the soul-world is such that he feels himself taken up into the activity of Moon, Mercury, Venus.

We must make a quite clear picture of this form of existence. Here on Earth we say: "As a man I have a head", activated chiefly by what might be called the middle brain —the pineal gland and so on. "In the middle of my body is my heart, and in my whole kidney system the organism for metabolism and movement." In the soul-world all this would have no meaning; we have laid it all aside. After death we say: "As a man I consist of what comes from the Moon-spirits on the Moon." This corresponds with saying on Earth: "I have a head." And whereas on Earth we say: "I have a heart in my breast"—which covers the whole breathing and circulatory system—in the soul-world we say: "I bear within me the forces of Venus." Again whereas on Earth we say: "I have a metabolic-limb system with all its organs," of which the chief is the kidney system, after death we have to say: "The forces coming from the Mercury beings live in me." Therefore on Earth we must say: "As man I am head, breast, lower body and limbs"; and after death: "As a man I am Moon, Venus, Mercury."

This corresponds entirely with our true inner existence during life. For our whole physical existence here on Earth depends upon how head, heart, and digestive system work together—everything turns on that. The slightest movement of the hand involves the action of head, heart and digestive system, for continuous changes in the relevant substances come into play. Our whole earthly existence takes its course in head, heart, limbs—to put it in a very summary way. So in the soul-world the activity of the Moon, Mercury and Venus forces within us fills our whole existence. And through this we are in fact carried back to a time when human beings were experiencing natural existence in long past epochs of human evolution—epochs to which I have often alluded during these lectures.

In those days people had a kind of instinctive vision, and I have already spoken here of certain types of this which can still be found. Even on Earth a man then had a presentiment of his connection, in life beyond the Earth, with Moon, Mercury and Venus. Why has this consciousness disappeared to-day? When anyone speaks of these deeply significant things which lie behind the veil of the physical world and can be spoken of only from the realm beyond the threshold, one naturally stirs up ill-feeling, or, to put it more elegantly, one arouses contemporary criticism. For to-day it is particularly difficult to put into words the truths of Initiation. It must either be done in such abstract concepts that people to-day will not realise what is meant, or terms that really belong to such truths must be used—and this makes many people down-right angry. One can understand this anger, for they are being told about a world they want to be rid of, a world they fear and hate. But this cannot prevent a start being made in speaking honestly of these matters in civilised circles. Were one to show great consideration—though it would not help us much —towards the people who hate Initiation-knowledge—not of course any of those sitting here but those in the world outside —one would have to say: As a man grows accustomed to life in the soul-world, he finds himself in conditions resembling an earlier condition on Earth, when he had instinctive spiritual knowledge of the truth, and in this knowledge, lived the forces of the Moon. In that way one might perhaps have gone half-way, quite respectably, towards the materialistic concepts of to-day; but it would have been put far too abstractly. If one is not afraid of the criticisms that will of course come from materialistic thinkers, one has to speak differently and say: When people were going through a far-off prehistoric epoch in earthly evolution—of which more is to be said later—even on Earth they were in the company of spiritual beings who were in direct connection with the Cosmos rather than with the Earth itself. We can say that divine Teachers, not earthly ones, directed the Mysteries and instructed human beings then on Earth.

In such remote ages these Teachers did not take on physi-cal bodies of flesh, but worked in their etheric bodies upon men. So that the highest Teachers in the Mysteries, to whom physically incorporated men stood merely as servants, were etheric and divine; but they dwelt among men on Earth. Hence we are expressing something very real when we say: Once, in a long past period of human evolution, divine-spiritual Beings dwelt on Earth together with men. They did not always make their presence known if someone, let us say, was simply going for a walk, but they did reveal themselves if a person was led to them in the right way through the servants of the Mystery-temples. This happened only in the Mysteries, and through the Mysteries these Beings became companions of earthly men. Since then they have withdrawn from the Earth to the Moon, where they now dwell as if in a cosmic citadel, not perceptible from earthly existence, within the Moon's inner being. Thus, when considering this inner existence of the Moon, we have to look upon it as a gathering of those Beings who once, in etheric bodies, were the great Teachers of men upon Earth. And really we should never look at the Moon without saying: Our one-time Teachers on Earth are now assembled there.

Nothing that comes to earthly men from the Moon is inherent in it, but only what is reflected by the Moon from the rest of the Cosmos. For the Moon reflects all cosmic activity in the same way that it reflects the light. Hence when we look at the Moon and see its light most clearly, this is really the least part of it. We are seeing a mirror of cosmic activities, not the inner life of the Moon.

Within the Moon dwell those Beings who once lived on Earth, and it is only during man's life in the soul-world, after death, that he again comes under their influence. It is these Beings who, in accordance with the judgment of the far-distant past, work correctively on what a man has done on Earth. After death, therefore, in our epoch, a man actually comes once more into relation with these Beings who formerly, as divine-spiritual Beings, educated and instructed him and all mankind on Earth.

When the human being has passed through this realm of the Moon, it is then his appointed task in the Cosmos to enter the Sun-existence. Whereas the first circle, the first completed spiral, has existence on the Moon for its central point, this spiral movement now takes a man a further step forward, and on leaving the realm of the Moon, he enters the realm of the Sun.

Any spatial diagram illustrating this process can be no more than illusory, for it all takes its course in the one-dimen-

sional, the supersensible. However, as we must use earthly
words, we can say: When a man has completed the first revolution in the realm of the Moon, he comes to the Sun
realm, and the Sun, the spiritual Sun, then stands in the same
relation to him as the Moon did previously. The man has
now to become a being who—on entering what in my book,
Theosophy, I called spirit-land, the spiritual realm of the Sun
—must transform his previous Moon-, Venus-, Mercury-, existence. He must in actual fact become a different being. In
earthly life he says: I am a being of head, heart, breast; a
being of metabolism and limbs. Immediately after death he
says: I am a being of Moon, Mercury, Venus. But then he
can no longer say this, for it would mean his having come
to a standstill in the spiritual world, between the soul-world
and the real world of the spirit. He has now to go through a
special metamorphosis even of his soul-spirit being and become what I may describe as follows: The Sun must be his
skin. Everything around must be Sun. As here on Earth our
physical body is wrapped in our skin, so now, on entering the
life of the spirit, we have to be clothed in a skin consisting entirely of the Sun's spiritual forces.

Now it is not easy to picture this, for on the Earth you
think: There is the Sun, shining down upon us; the Sun is in
the centre and sheds its rays all around. On entering the realm
of the spiritual Sun we find the Sun to be no longer in a definite place—it is everywhere. A man is then within the Sun;
it shines in upon him from the periphery, and is, in truth,
the spiritual skin of the entity he has become. Moreover, within
the realm of the spiritual Sun, we have what must be described
as organs. In the same way that in earthly life we have head,
heart, limbs, and, immediately after death, Moon, Mercury,
Venus, so, after that, we have organs which we must attribute
to Mars, Jupiter, Saturn.

These are then our inner organs, just as heart, pineal gland,
kidneys, are on Earth. All this has gone through a metamorphosis into the spiritual and these new organs, not fully
formed when first we leave the soul-world and enter the
world of spirit, now have to be gradually developed. For this

purpose we do not describe one circle only in the Sun-existence, as in our Moon-existence, but three. In the first circle the spiritual Mars organ is developed; in the second, the Jupiter organ, and the Saturn organ in the last circle. If we compare them with earthly periods of time, we find that these three circles are traversed much more slowly, about twelve times more slowly than the relatively fast Moon circle. And during this whole journey, while a man is living in the world of spiritual spheres and participating in its forces, he is continually active. Just as we are active here with the forces of nature, so there we are active with the forces, the Beings, of the higher Hierarchies, whose physical manifestation in the surrounding starry heavens is only an outer reflection, as with the Sun and Moon.

In order to find his way from the realm of the Moon to that of the Sun, however, a man must have the guidance to which I have already referred. We have seen how, in the most ancient epochs of mankind, Beings lived on Earth who have since withdrawn, entrenching themselves. as it were, in the cosmic stronghold of the Moon. They are the Beings with whom a man, after death, first enters into a relationship. But these Beings have had successors who, in the epochs after the ancient Hyperborean period, appeared on Earth from time to time. In the East they have been called Bodhisattvas. Although they have always made their appearance embodied as men, yet they are the successors of the Beings now entrenched on the Moon, and their life is passed in community with these Beings. There lie the springs of their strength, the sources of their thoughts. And they were the Beings who once acted as the guides of mankind. Through the teaching they gave on Earth, men were enabled to have the strength, on coming to the end of their journey through the Moon-sphere, to pass over into the realm of the Sun.

In future lectures we shall see how, in the course of man's earthly evolution, this has become impossible, and how the Christ Being had to descend from the Sun to carry out the Mystery of Golgotha so that mankind, through the teachings of that Mystery, should be given sufficient force to make the crossing from the soul-world to spirit-land, from Moon-sphere to Sun-sphere.

In the ancient days of Earth evolution, the Moon-influence was closely connected with the Earth, and cared for its spiritual element, with the participation, direct or indirect, of the Bodhisattvas. Then, when the time was ripe, after the first third of the fourth post-Atlantean epoch had expired, the effects of the Mystery of Golgotha, the working of the Christ, came in. This work of the Christ was surrounded by the twelvefold activity of the Bodhisattvas, indicated—though indeed it was a reality—in the twelve Apostles. Thus the Christ, incorporated in the body of Jesus, is the power who, coming from spiritual existence in the Sun, has now united Himself with the Earth.

If we look up to the Moon with the desire to understand it, rather than merely to gaze at it with our soul and spirit clouded by materialism, and if we realise it to be a gathering of beings pointing to the past evolution of the Earth, then we must look up in the same way to the Sun. The Sun is a gathering of those Beings who point to the future of Earth-evolution and now also to the present, and whose great representative is the Christ, who passed through the Mystery of Golgotha. Through as much as human beings absorb on Earth in their relation to that Mystery, so will their entrance into the spiritual land of the Sun be facilitated, so that they are enabled to take up inwardly the Mars organ in the sphere of Mars, the Jupiter organ in the Jupiter-sphere, and in the sphere of Saturn the corresponding Saturn organ. This is accomplished in threefold circles which take their course far more slowly than that of the Moon; yet this also underlies world-evolution. The complete fulfilment of what I have just been describing—the development into Mars man, Jupiter man, Saturn man—will come about only in the future. During our present epoch we can make only the circle of the Mars region after death, through the activity of world-forces; after that we are unable to do more than touch on the Jupiter region. We have to go through many earthly lives before being able—between death and rebirth—to enter fully the Jupiter region and, later still, that of Saturn.

In order that man, though not yet able to enter the Jupiter region, may receive, between death and a new birth, something of the forces of Jupiter and also of Saturn, many planetoids are interpersed between Mars and Jupiter; in their outer aspect they are constantly being discovered by the astronomers. They make up the region which in its spiritual aspect is experienced by a man after death because he cannot yet reach Jupiter. They have the remarkable characteristic of being spiritual colonies, as it were, of beings from Jupiter and Saturn who have withdrawn there. And before a man is ripe for existence on Earth, he can find in this region of the planetoids, which are there for that purpose, a kind of preparatory substitute, before he is able to enter the region of Jupiter and Saturn. At present, therefore, by the time a man has gone through death and rebirth, he has achieved his Mars-organisation, and has absorbed those Jupiter and Saturn forces to be found in the colonised regions of the planetoids. With the after-effects of this—we still have to learn about them—the human being embarks on another earthly life.

How this life between death and a new birth, which I have now described in relation to the world of the stars, can be further characterised, we shall hear to-morrow.

XI

Experience of the World's Past

If we look back on the descriptions given yesterday, we shall be aware that man, living through successive times after death—and we have to use the word "time" in relation to physical conditions—comes first of all to the realm of the Moon Beings, and then passes on to that of the Sun Beings. The Moon Beings still belong to earthly-existence in a certain sense and the experiences a man goes through under their influence in the soul-world are indeed cosmic memories of earthly existence. He has experiences also of his own earthly life, though now in a backwards direction, and these are united with the judgments of the Cosmos, as I called them yesterday. These cosmic judgments are made known to men after death through the Moon Beings. We then come under the influence of these Beings, and it is they who cause the judgments to flow into us, in the same way as those that flow into us, here on Earth, from minerals, plants and animals. So we can say : On entering spiritual-cosmic existence after death, a man gains his first glimpse into such cosmic perceptions as still proceed from Beings once connected with the Earth. We have already had occasion to speak of how these Beings, before taking up their abode in the cosmic stronghold of the Moon, were Teachers of human beings in the ancient Mysteries. Hence, what a man once experienced on Earth, in primeval times, he now experiences when journeying through the soul-world, under the influence of those Beings who have been raised—we might perhaps say—to become inhabitants of the Moon. We can truly speak of them in this way if sufficient consideration is given to what was said in my last lecture. These inhabitants of the Moon, under the leadership of the one-time Teachers of mankind, judge quite differently from the way things are judged by people on Earth. For people on Earth, in their life between birth and death, are now approaching a stage completed by the Moon-dwellers in long past ages.

Reckoning by earthly years, we must say that the inhabitants of the Moon, when on Earth, accomplished quite 15,000 years ago what human beings still have to do. More than 15,000 years have passed since these Moon inhabitants acquired the power of making judgments which bring together the naturalistic and the moral.

We on Earth keep our naturalistic judgments separate, and when giving an opinion about a stone or an animal we leave morality aside. We say: "Nature follows only an amoral necessity." But this is not true of the world as a *whole*. Even though we may consider that moral judgments are not applicable to individual animals, or to plants, or to minerals above all, in their separate forms of existence, yet the very fact of their creation, of their being in the world at all, is entirely the result of cosmic moral judgment.

Now these Moon-dwellers already judge in terms of cosmic morality. Therefore, when we have passed through the gate of death and are together with them, we must listen to all the Cosmos has to say about what we have thought, wished, felt, willed and done on Earth. Our entire earthly life is exposed to the light of cosmic judgment, and we learn the value our deeds have for the whole great universe.

From these lessons we develop the impulse to complete, to correct, or in some way to set right, during our next life on Earth, whatever we have done either to help or to hinder the evolution of the world. And so, while thus under the influence of the Moon Beings, we take up the impulses for our future destiny—for our karma, as oriental wisdom has always called it. These impulses are thus absorbed while the human being is still under the influence of dwellers in the Moon, who are able to tell him how much his earthly deeds and thoughts are worth for the Cosmos.

The spiritual Beings of the higher world, in whose neighbourhood a man lives while under the influence of the Moon-dwellers, are those grouped together in my *Occult Science* as the Hierarchy of Angels, Archangels, Archai. Of the ranks of

Beings whose realm a man enters after death, they are the
first who do not have to live through a phase of earthly em-
bodiment. On their side, they stand in close connection with
the Beings of the still higher Hierarchies. But it is with this
Hierarchy of Angels, Archangels and Archai that a man is
essentially concerned during his Moon existence after death,
while the higher Hierarchies are still beyond his ken.

The judgments of the Angels are especially important for the
deeds of individual men, and it is thus from the Angels that
a man learns the value his deeds have in the Cosmos as a
whole. From the Archangels he learns more about the value
of what he has done in connection with the language he
speaks, with the people to whom he belongs, and from this
source also come impulses which work into his further destiny,
his karma. From the Archai he learns what value his actions
during a given period on Earth will have for the time when
he has to descend once more from spiritual heights into
earthly existence.

By means of all that a man can achieve in this way if—and
I beg you to bear the following in mind—he has rightly prepared himself for life after death through the impulses he is
able to receive on Earth, and particularly (as we shall see later)
through his attitude towards the great leaders of mankind, he
can then find the way over from the sphere of the Moon-
dwellers to the sphere of the Sun-dwellers.

The inhabitants of the Moon we already know as those
Beings who once dwelt on Earth and were in close connection
with it. In a very, very much earlier age this was true also
of the inhabitants of the Sun; they, too, participated in
earthly affairs.

On coming to the realm of the Moon-dwellers it is quite
clear to a man that he is meeting Beings who once dwelt with
him on Earth. And when he enters the realm of the Sun Beings, something like a powerful cosmic memory of a primeval
age comes over him—an age which in *Occult Science* you will
find described from another point of view. He is taken
possession of by something like a memory of an infinitely
ancient time, when the Sun, with its inhabitants, was still one

with the Earth. After death, therefore, we make our way through the spiritual Cosmos by growing into, as it were, two spiritual cosmic regions where we meet those Beings with whom, at one time, when we lived on Earth as quite different beings, we were closely associated.

So it is that by going through these experiences between death and a new birth we look back in grand, mighty memories on the evolution of the Earth in the Cosmos. Whereas a man, while here on Earth, goes through only part of human evolution, between death and rebirth he goes through part of cosmic evolution, part of the evolution of the universe. Those Beings who inhabit the Sun are such that in far distant times they had already risen above the experiences possible for earthly beings, and above those possible for the Beings of the Moon.

On reaching the realm of the Sun Beings, a man enters a sphere of the highest wisdom, where he can live only if on Earth he has prepared himself sufficiently for it.

Now I said yesterday that on passing from the soul-world into the land of spirit, or, as we must express it to-day, from the sphere of the Moon-dwellers to that of the Sun-dwellers, a man proceeds more slowly in his journeyings through the Cosmos. Whereas the circling of the Moon takes about a third of his earthly lifetime, the next rounds, the circling of Mars, of Jupiter, and of Saturn—I mentioned yesterday how these rounds are not completed—takes a more leisurely course, twelve times slower than the circling of the Moon.

If now we reckon up the actual time, we arrive at the following result. We must start from the original plan decreed for human beings by the Cosmos. Then we find that a man goes through the Moon period in a third of the time he has spent on Earth. If we allow for the fact that at the beginning of life more time is spent in sleep, and add on the time given to sleep in later life, we find that a man needs approximately thirty years to accomplish the first cycle, that of the Moon. Each of the following cycles takes twelve times as long, or 360 years for each cycle. If we follow a man in his further journeying through the worlds, we find him going

through three cycles. He does not reach Saturn, but has to go
through the cycles in the way originally decided. He then has
to go backwards through the three again. Thus he completes
three cycles in an outward direction and, on returning towards
his next earthly life, another three backwards, making six in
all. We then have the time originally intended for man. I
shall still have to speak of how things are different for human
beings to-day; but according to the original cosmic decrees,
the time was 2,160 years.

What do these 2,160 years signify? You have only to recall
that the position of the Sun at the vernal equinox moves forward year by year. In recent centuries it has advanced from
the Ram to the Fishes, and approximately in 25,920 years—
or close on 26,000 years—the Sun travels round the whole
zodiacal circle, and the twelfth part of this is 2,160 years. In
2,160 years the Sun progresses from one sign of the Zodiac to
the next. It was originally decreed that a man should return
to Earth when the Sun had thus moved on.

When we consider the inner reasons for this number, and
compare it with what from I said from another point of view
in *Occult Science,* those who have read the book will remember that the time taken by the Sun to pass from one sign of
the Zodiac to the next was given there as the original length
of the interval between a man's incarnations. If we look at
this from two sides—more outwardly, from the cosmic aspect,
as in *Occult Science,* and then from the side of man's inner
life that we are dealing with to-day—the two numbers are
identical. Such things should be noticed; and it will be found
that whenever in Spiritual Science a correct judgment is made
from one point of view, and then another correct judgment
from a quite different point of view, the two judgments are inwardly in agreement.

Anyone judging Spiritual Science from the ordinary standpoint of to-day will quite possibly ask: "What is there to
support this Spiritual Science of yours? Our natural science
rests upon observation, experiment; that is the firm ground
from which we start." But one might just as well say: "As
earthly man I stand on firm ground, and a rock, too, has

solid ground beneath it—like everything else on Earth. As for you astronomers—it is really fantastic for you to tell us that the Earth is floating freely in celestial space. If you want to be reasonable, you must say that the Earth, like any great mass of rock, is somewhere resting on firm ground." That is virtually the same as accusing Anthroposophy of having no firm ground to stand on. Naturally, people would appear foolish, even to themselves, were they to say that the Earth has something to rest on, but they do not see how foolish it is not to realise that Spiritual Science, which is carried by its own inner resources, just as the heavenly bodies move by their own impulses, cannot rest on the ground of experiment and explanation. Were they only to be consistent in their judgments, they would see how, in the Spiritual Science intended here, every step is made with the utmost exactitude, and full accountability is taken for every statement concerning the world and the beings of the world.

Thus, after death, a man enters a world which he at first experiences in common with souls who, like himself, have entered the spiritual worlds through the gate of death after an earthly life. A man thus grows familiar with the sphere of disembodied human beings and continues with them the earthly relations experienced spiritually at night.

But we have also seen how a man finds himself in the company of other spiritual Beings, the inhabitants of the Moon who were once dwelling with him on the Earth, and how, afterwards, he ascends to the community on the Sun. These Sun-dwellers also were once inhabitants of the Earth together with human beings, though in times far more remote. Here a man's first meeting is with the Beings who constitute the second Hierarchy, described in my *Occult Science* as Exusiai, Dynamis, Kyriotetes. These are the Beings with whom he has to work in order that he may be able to manifest in his next earthly life the cosmically elaborated karma derived from his earlier lives on Earth.

Having passed through the realm of the Moon-dwellers, a

man knows—not with earthly thoughts but with cosmic ones —what in a cosmic sense he has done wrong; he realises the worth for cosmic evolution as a whole of all he has done, thought and felt. But he cannot prepare his new earthly life with cosmic thoughts alone. Therefore in the Moon-sphere he comes to know what he is destined to be in his next earthly existence, though the actual preparations for it cannot be made at that stage. For this, he has to rise to the sphere of the Sun, where live the Beings who, no longer having to concern themselves with earthly existence, are occupied with the affairs of our whole planetary system.

So a man's experience of the Cosmos embraces two spiritual regions, together with the spiritual Beings dwelling in them. It embraces the soul-world of the Moon-dwellers, and the more extensive population of the spirit region. Whereas the Moon-dwellers, because they were closely connected with the Earth in comparatively recent times, have united their interests with the peoples of the Earth, and while the Moon is in a sense only a cosmic colony, occupied with and orientated towards earthly affairs, the Sun-sphere, whose dwellers live under the leadership of the Exusiai, Dynamis, Kyriotetes, is a cosmic whole, concerned with the affairs of the entire planetary system—Mars, Saturn, Jupiter, Venus and so on, including the Earth and the Moon.

On coming into this vast sphere of the Sun, where our interests are substantially widened, we are able to work with the Exusiai, Dynamis and Kyriotetes on preparing the spirit-germ of a physical body which can then be born for us from human parents. No parents could ever produce a suitable physical body were it not prepared during long periods through work carried out in co-operation with the highest, most sublime spiritual Beings in the spiritual Cosmos. Our essential work there—a work far greater and more comprehensive than anything achieved during our little life on Earth—is to concern ourselves, together with Beings of a higher degree, with all that takes place among these Beings as spiritual events, just as here there are natural events; with all that takes place in them as art of the spirit, just as here we have the art of nature. All this finally enables us to bring together what has thus been worked upon into a great, spiritual, archetypal picture which is the spirit-germ—as it were the foreshadowing—of what will later be born on Earth as our physical body.

When a man, having completed the three circles, starts on the return journey, his interest in earthly affairs revives. Then —still many years before birth—he looks down on the successive generations in earthly evolution, at the end of which will stand his father and his mother. As soon as he makes this complete change of direction in the Cosmos, he begins to focus his attention upon the Earth. He watches many preceding generations of his ancestry, one after another, until, centuries later, his parents are born. To them he can send down the potent, far-reaching spirit-germ, diminished in size, of his future physical body, so that this spirit-germ can be united with the physical embryo in the body of the mother.

The spirit-germ is at first majestic and great, like the Cosmos itself. While a man is making his return journey to the physical world, and watching the generations through which his parents descend, and while from the spiritual world he is actively concerned with this sequence of generations, the germ becomes smaller and smaller—until at last it arrives back in the Mars-sphere, the actual sphere of the Sun, and then, passing quickly through the Moon-sphere, it descends to its next life on Earth.

Some time before the man himself descends as a being of soul, he sends down in advance this spirit-germ, so that what he has prepared for his physical body enters the physical world before him. On completing his work for the new earthly life, he is able to enter into a different relation with the cosmos—a relation indeed to the whole cosmic ether. And, as the final act in his descent, he draws from spiritual worlds, out of the whole world-ether, the forces to form his etheric body.

When a man has already sent down the spirit-germ for his physical body—that is, when the spirit-germ has at last descended to the parents at the end of its long journey down from the spiritual world—the man himself, still in the spiritual world, gathers ether around him there, and for a short time becomes a being of Ego, astral body and ether, the ether having been drawn together from the world-ether. It is not until after conception, during the third or fourth week of the embryonic period, that the human being unites himself with the organism that has been formed by combining the spirit-germ with the physical germ, and bestows upon it the etheric body drawn from the world-ether. Man then becomes a being composed of physical body, an etheric body drawn together in the last moments of his cosmic existence, and the astral body and Ego which have gone through the life between death and rebirth.

Thus, after experiencing the purely spiritual, a man descends to yet another existence in the physical world.

From what has been said you will have gathered that while passing through life in the world between death and a new birth, we experience in memory past ages of the Earth's evolution—the evolution of worlds, one might call it. The world-memories thus lived through become a man's deeds, for he does something with these memories, in cooperation with the higher Beings of whom I have already spoken and will speak further. What he carries out, while active in memory and remembering in activity, gives a significant perspective into the past of the Earth and of the world.

The experiences he goes through while in connection with the inhabitants of the Moon conjures up in his soul a time during which he passed through earlier lives on Earth in a similar relation to them as now. He surveys a series of earthly lives resembling those of the present. He then looks further back to a time when, even while on Earth, he was more closely connected with the present dwellers on the Moon; to a time from which he is separated by what geologists call the Ice Age. He looks back to a phase in earthly evolution you will find described in my books as the Atlantean age. But he penetrates still further back to what is called the age of Lemuria, when man is still to be found on Earth, though under quite different conditions. He was not yet so closely bound to the Earth that he trod it with his feet; he lived more as an etheric being in the environment of the Earth, in its atmosphere. This he could do because at that time the atmosphere consisted mainly of a watery solution that has now been distributed between seas and continents, together with solutions of other substances that have since become the solid earth of to-day. Hence he lived more in the Earth's circumference during the age—here again names are unimportant—called the Lemurian, which corresponds to what natural scientists call, with some justification, the oldest period of the Earth.

We then look back to an age when man was still associated with the Sun Beings, with the inhabitants of the Sun, before in the course of cosmic evolution the Sun separated from the Earth. This does not mean looking back to an age when, as described in *Occult Science*, the Earth itself went through its Sun period—the second age in the evolution of the Earth—but to the recapitulation in earthly existence of that cosmic age. But this recapitulation does come into view. And so a man's knowledge, when supplemented by what he is able to experience between death and a new birth, becomes cosmological knowledge. Earth-evolution advances through repeated stages, in conjunction with the results of human deeds carried out together with higher Beings. The Earth's past, in its connection with the whole planetary system—Sun, Moon, and all the planets dependent on them—becomes apparent in the deeds of men. Out of it a man shapes the part of the future for which he is responsible—his next earthly life. At the same time, however, he is involved in the preparation of future worlds, the Jupiter, Venus and Vulcan existences, for into each of these in turn the Earth existence will eventually be transformed.

If we look deeply into such matters, we can understand how ancient cosmic times were part of the world-evolution of the Earth. We look back indeed into an age when the Moon-dwellers of to-day provided the instructors of mankind. Then, together with the latest great instructors, they withdrew into the cosmic stronghold of the Moon.

Over and over again on Earth, however, men were born with the capacity to remain throughout their karmic life in close connection with the experiences of those who now dwell on the Moon. Born again and again in the course of world-evolution, they were like ambassadors of the great community within the Moon. They appeared among the people of the Earth during the first, second and third post-Atlantean culture-epochs and in the East they developed a lofty civilisation. These ambassadors of the Moon were called Bodhisattvas. They dwelt on Earth as men, but in them lived on the spiritual teaching that had been given directly by the great Moon teachers on Earth.

Now there are often times in the universe when the inhabitants of the Moon, because they are more nearly connected with the inhabitants of the Sun than with those of the Earth, develop a particularly intimate relation with these Sun-dwellers, so that, indirectly, through the Moon ambassadors—called in the East the Bodhisattvas—the wisdom of the Sun was able to reach men on Earth in the older oriental civilisations. Because of the progress made in the evolution of the Earth, it then became necessary that earthly civilisation should no longer be nourished, as it were, by the Moon Beings only. The whole evolution of the Earth would have had to take a course different from the one prescribed by cosmic wisdom, if only the Moon ambassadors had figured in it. For this reason there came about the great, momentous event we call the Mystery of Golgotha.

Whereas in more ancient times it was the Moon ambassadors who, to a certain extent, brought the Sun wisdom to Earth, it was the Leader of the Sun Beings Himself, foremost in the ranks of Sun Spirits, who, through the Mystery of Golgotha, came down to Earth into the body of the man Jesus. Through this, quite different conditions arose for the evolution of the Earth. The wisdom of the Sun-dwellers was brought into it as impulse by Christ Jesus; and under this impulse the further course of Earth-evolution must therefore proceed.

At the time of the Mystery of Golgotha, so much Moon

wisdom was still spread over the whole Earth that as Gnosis, as Pistis Sophia—which was old Moon wisdom—it was able to understand the nature of the Christ. Gnosis was essentially an endeavour to grasp His whole spiritual significance. But Gnosis has been entirely rooted out. In the phase of evolution which led to a temporary lack of understanding of the Mystery of Golgotha, the first act was the rooting out of the Gnosis—down, almost, to the very writings of its opponents.

Imagine that nothing were left of our present Anthroposophy except what its opponents have written about it, and this will give you some idea of what people know of Gnosis from external sources. Their knowledge is limited to the opinions of its opponents, perhaps to some acquaintance with the Pistis Sophia and so on, which they don't understand. That is all they know of the Gnosis, which is indeed a gift of the Moon, out of the past, to the first centuries of Christianity—particularly the first four centuries, for after that it was no longer understood. It was what could be said out of the old Moon wisdom, out of the Moon Logos, to the Sun Logos who had come to Earth—said, that is, to the Christ. Anyone aware of this can really understand the Gnosis, which has been greatly misjudged, and of which such strange things are said to-day.

It is not possible, however, for matters to remain thus, for the evolution of the Earth must continue. We have to progress from the old wisdom of the Moon to a new Sun wisdom, for which we must learn to have an immediate understanding. To-morrow I shall have to describe how it was essentially the old Moon wisdom—after it had come virtually to an end—which still spoke to human beings through a form of Yoga breathing, through a changed breathing process. It was a striving after the old wisdom of the Moon.

This Yoga cult is no longer suitable for Western people; they must attain to Imagination. For civilisation in general, that is the necessary next step—the endeavour to come to Imagination. But there are all sorts of obstacles, and this means that the evolution of human civilisation can advance only if a new impulse from the spirit is accepted. This depends on intimate human destinies. When Bodhisattvas appeared, they never found people generally hostile. Those ancient times may often appear to us outwardly as gruesome and terrible, but it was always possible to meet with good will when bringing impulses from the spiritual worlds. Hence the Bodhisattvas found men ready to receive the old Moon Logos—the reflection, that is, of the Sun Logos. But it will never again be possible to speak to mankind in that old way.

The old Moon wisdom, the old Moon Logos, however, cannot cease—like everything else, it has to progress. But it will have to be understood through the Sun Word, which, having lost its last legacy in the Gnosis, must be re-discovered. It will be impossible to speak to people in the true language of the Sun until they bring good will to meet it. Until they do so, they will wait in vain for the coming of a successor to the Bodhisattvas of old, for that depends upon whether human beings welcome him with understanding.

To-day there is a deep rift between the humanity of the East and the humanity of the West. And those who do not go deeply enough into these matters cannot see how East and West are divided, and how the East is waiting for the new Bodhisattva to bring them in his own way something of which the West has only the vaguest idea. The nationalistic struggles of to-day have not yet been sufficiently overcome throughout the Earth by the universal consciousness which must flow essentially from the Christ impulse. Men will never discover how to rise to this common humanity, this genuine Christ impulse, and will never be able to understand what a potential Bodhisattva would have to say, until they have developed enough spiritual longing in them to create a bridge for a world-wide understanding between East and West.

I am touching here on a theme we must go further into to-morrow—a theme that will show how different the present time is from the days when man waited expectantly for the coming of a Bodhisattva. Now, before the Bodhisattva can speak to men, he has himself to wait until they are ready to understand the words he will use, for men have now entered the epoch of freedom.

This entry into the epoch of freedom, in relation to our present theme, will be a subject for to-morrow. But all that mankind has to go through, in order to find the innermost impulse in the spiritual world above, is connected with many apparently insignificant cultural systems and symptoms of our civilisation.

Forgive me for intermingling the great with the trivial, but trivial symptoms can sometimes throw light on the great. A few days ago I said that in this region, where Imaginations take so firm a hold on the spirit, we get the disturbance of motor-cars. I added that I was not saying anything against motor-cars, for in Anthroposophy we cannot express reactionary views, and when necessary I am obviously very fond of travelling by car myself. One must take the world as it is. But anything one-sided must always be balanced by its opposite. Thus there is no harm in motoring—provided we take it, and everything of that kind, with a heart attuned to the spiritual world. Then, if other things besides cars come to disturb us, we shall be able to press on by dint of our own strength and freedom, for freedom had to come, and it must lead us back to the Bodhisattva.

Human beings will be able to help themselves, where things are concerned that do us good service mechanically. It can truly be said that men will be able to help themselves in face of what comes upon them in the way of cars, typewriters, and so on.

With gramophones, however, it is different—forgive me for concluding on such an apparently trivial note. With gramophones, art is being thrust down into a machine. When people develop a passion for such a thing—which is really a mechanising of what comes down to us as a shadow of the spiritual—when they show enthusiasm for the kind of thing represented by gramophones, then in this connection they no longer have the power to help themselves. At this point the Gods have to help.

Now the Gods are merciful, and to-day our hope for the future progress of human civilisation must be that the Gods in their mercy will themselves come to the rescue where— as in the case of the gramophone—men's taste has gone astray.

XII

The Evolution of the World in Connection with the Evolution of Man

In the course of our observations about the world and about man, we have seen how he bears within him—if only in picture form—the past of the world, and how it is possible for him, by gradual training, to conjure up these pictures. In our ordinary daytime consciousness there is nothing of all this, but only memories of our experiences during earthly life. When, however, a man applies this ordinary consciousness to following the path I have indicated, then, as his spiritual consciousness grows clearer and clearer, more and more of the past evolution of worlds arises within him. And we have found how this experience of the past has to be renewed between death and rebirth.

We can therefore say: When things that are not perceptible for the senses become so for Imagination, a man looks back beyond the memories of his current life. He looks back on everything that has gone to shape him, on the forces of growth and nourishment which have formed him from within—all of which proceeds from the spirit.

And further, in Inspiration a man looks into pre-earthly existence, but not only into his own. We have seen already how he reaches out beyond the cosmic island of the Earth to the great cosmic ocean in which the stars have their dwelling, and he finds that the stars then become for him the dwelling-places of spiritual Beings.

Then, when Intuition arises, a man gazes back into past lives on Earth. At the same time the whole past life of the world comes into the range of his vision. He is, in actual fact, born out of the whole world; the whole world lives in his physical, etheric and astral bodies, and—during earthly existence—least of all as yet in his Ego. All this is included in a man, working and weaving within him. As human beings we bear within us the whole past evolution of the world, upon which countless generations of the spirit have worked. We bear this divine work in the building up of our organs, and in the forces weaving and living in them; we bear it within us when those organs flower into perception and thought. We carry within us the work that has gone into the whole past evolution of the world. When now, after we have—at least in thought—sharpened our vision into the past, we look out at the world surrounding us here on Earth, we see with ordinary consciousness only as much as the senses offer and whatever our intellect can make of our sense-observations. Behind the realm of sense-perception lies the all-embracing life of the spirit—a life active in all colours and sounds of nature, in everything we experience as warmth or cold, in every aspect of natural phenomena that can affect us as human beings.

Besides the physical nature revealed to the senses, there is a concealed spiritual nature—a hidden spiritual environment. This surrounding spiritual world, of which only the veriest surface is apparent to sense-perception, carries even now in its womb man's future evolution. Just as we bear within us in mighty pictures the entire past and are ourselves the outcome of those pictures, so in the concealed life of nature there works and weaves that which, in its further unfolding as world-evolution, will bring us our future. Thus we can set before us these weighty words: Man bears within him the past of the world; the outer world is the bearer of his future.

These are the two fundamental principles upon which world-evolution and human evolution are founded. And indeed they come to expression in individual human life. There is a great difference between all that tends more towards a man's head-organisation, and all that has more to do with the rest of his body. To put it rather crudely, one might say: Forces work up from the heart towards the head organisation and bring about the particular configuration of the head, with its covering of hard skull. This is filled with the most wonderful construction in all the world—the convolutions and interweavings of the human brain, in which the senses are embedded.

Everything living in these forces, all that flows to a man's head from his breast and heart, is an outcome of the past. This could become what it now is in man only because— as we have already said— innumerable divine generations of the spirit have worked upon it, through the metamorphoses of cosmic-planetary bodies. In my *Occult Science* I have pointed out how a Saturn-evolution, a Sun-evolution, a Moon-evolution, preceded in turn the Earth-evolution in which we are living and during which the Saturn-, Sun- and Moon-evolutions have been recapitulated. We are now rather past the middle of the actual Earth-evolution, the evolution of man on Earth.

The forces which through long ages have been gradually developing, under the influence of divine generations of the spirit, all live in the physical body of earthly man, and stream from his heart up to his head. All that you bear continually in your physical, etheric, astral and Ego, as a streaming up from the centre of your being to your head, has been prepared and worked upon by generations of Gods through immeasurable periods of time. And the last element which lives in these up-streaming forces—though people to-day are still unconscious of it—is that which expresses itself as a man's karma—the past of his own Ego during his lives on Earth.

We can put it in this way. If we penetrate deeply into these forces of cosmic memory, we come first to karma; then to the various stages of Earth-evolution; after that to the metamorphoses, the planetary transformations which the Earth went through before becoming the actual Earth. Before the Earth could come into being, there had to be a cosmic body, Saturn, consisting only of tenuous warmth. Saturn had then to pass away before rising to a new existence as that Sun of which our Sun, now seen outside in cosmic space, is the residue. At that time the Sun was a cosmic body consisting of air alone; this again had to pass away and give place to a cosmic body consisting of water—the old Moon. Then the Moon in turn gave place to the firm mineral substance of the Earth, on which man, as an earthly being, could begin to evolve.

But just as we have these upward-striving forces, so do we bear within us forces with a downward trend. They have a kind of central point in the heart, and the circulating blood carries both forces to the movements of our limbs. These forces are active in every movement of our hands; when you take hold of anything, or perform any ordinary earthly action, they enter into every move you make. They do not now belong to the past; they belong to the hidden world around us. They will be taken up into the womb of the past—which will become the past only in the future—when a man goes through the gate of death, and exchanges his earthly existence for life among the stars. These are the forces in which a man's future is prepared.

The future comes about through the interplay of these forces with the forces concealed in external nature. Thus the world bears man's future within its own evolution. There is a sharp distinction in him between these upper forces and the lower ones. The knowledge that can be acquired after passing the Guardian of the Threshold bring out this distinction strongly.

For ordinary consciousness, everything below the heart remains unconscious. This does not mean that it is any less fully imbued with consciousness, but this is a consciousness beyond our normal reach to-day. Hence what a man experiences inwardly differs from the content of his consciousness. He is conscious only of what is on the surface, rising like an island out of his other experiences.

When we are able to penetrate further into the human being, we can see how he is still endowed to-day with these subconscious forces. We can then see how a man performs some deed which, for that moment of his earthly life, causes him pleasure and satisfaction—his head is satisfied. He may for some reason have done a thoroughly bad thing, but his head is satisfied, and the implications of his action evade his ordinary consciousness. But although his head may be perfectly satisfied, the hand that carries out the action is subconsciously affected by it—and the subconscious is really another form of consciousness—and his hand quivers. The quivering may be outwardly imperceptible, but in the etheric and astral bodies it becomes an actual trembling. So we can see inwardly how a man may be satisfied in his head with some deed that subconsciously causes a trembling in the astral and etheric organs connected with his arms or legs. In the satisfaction given to the head by a bad deed, consciousness is—we might say—benumbed; but another form of consciousness arises in the depths of a man's being, and there the deed causes a trembling.

In this trembling, future karma is being prepared. It is a trembling in face of the forces concealed in nature, forces of the hidden world. The trembling presages the judgment that will be passed upon the man by the Beings of the stars, when, from this litle island of the Earth, he goes out into the wide starry ocean.

To sum this up : Within the human being, in diverse ways, both the past and the future of the world are living—even in the external form of his physical body. A man's head-organisation, that most wonderful, most perfect product of world-evolution, is to a great extent broken up, even spiritually, when he passes through the gate of death. On the other hand, his lower organisation, though merely physical in outward appearance, is in reality a physical picture of that which lives as soul and spirit in the arms and hands, in the whole metabolic-limb system. Through this system, through all you can see as flesh and blood shaped into arms and hands, spiritual forces flow. In a future life on Earth these forces will flow through the organs that bring about the movements of the upper and lower jaw. The bones of the head in their plastic formation will then be the transformed bones of arms and legs—naturally I mean the spiritual part of these, for the physical falls away. That which now constitutes your arms and legs will become in your next incarnation—to speak in terms of forces and dynamics—the configuration of your head. Hence the physical organisation itself affords a reflection of how a man has gone through earthly life. Anyone who studies in the right way the artistic shaping of a man's head can see in the very form of his head how he used his arms and hands in his dealings with other people and with the external world during his previous earthly life. For the deeds of arms and legs in one earthly incarnation live on in the formation of the head in the next incarnation. Ordinary phrenology is superficial in giving all kinds of intellectual interpretations of the shape of the head. But behind this is a deep, occult phrenology which considers the individuality of each man and does not conform to general rules—a phrenology that out of Intuitions is able to discern how the formations of a man's head have been prepared by the outcome of his movements, his behaviour and his actions during a previous life on Earth.

That, then, is how the human being stands before us to-day, and before himself, showing in what he has become how divine generations of the spirit have worked upon him through immeasurable periods of time. Naturally one can only indicate in outline how a man's life to-day illustrates in pictures all that these generations of the Gods have done for him, and for all mankind, through the metamorphoses of Earth-evolution—Saturn, Sun and Moon.

Let us take first three particularly significant impulses in the earthly life of human beings. If one looks quite simply, with ordinary consciousness, at the wonders revealed in the progressive development of the human being from the first days of his life, we can at least gain some idea, some feeling, of the tremendous depths out of which the soul and spirit struggle during those first days and weeks in order to give an increasingly definite form to much that in the infant is still formless; and then gradually to bring under control the chaotic movements of arms and legs. We come to feel that we are being shown how a spiritual activity, present in the endless depths of the hidden life of nature, is expressing itself in the human body. And we can say : There is nothing on Earth so wonderful to watch as the unfolding of the inner human being within the outer, during the development of a child in the very first years of its life. If we know how to watch this with true artistic-religious insight, then all that can be seen there, and the humility we can feel in face of this revelation of the spiritual, surpass all other artistic, scientific or religious impressions that can be received from the outer world.

But let us single out three things in the development of a child. In ordinary life we say : The child is learning to walk. In fact, this is something wonderful. In this learning to walk an extraordinary amount of movement is involved. All the limbs are called into play when, in order to stand erect, the child raises itself out of the position where its spine is parallel with the surface of the Earth. We take this for granted as something obvious, but it marks the moment in the child's life when it is learning to give all its forces a different orientation on Earth, and, with the help of the symmetry of those forces and its own inner balance, is learning to establish itself within the Cosmos as a whole. At the same time, we are really watching how a human being is growing out of the animal world. For this is a moment that an animal can never experience. It remains essentially with its spine parallel to the Earth; for if it pulls itself upright, as the ape does, this is contrary to its natural organisation.

If we are to form a true conception of man, we must be able to see in the right light this learning to walk on the part of the child. Scientists have compared the bones of the human being with those of the animal, and have found them to be animal bones transformed, and men's muscles to be animal muscles transformed—and so on. Let this be so with every organ; the difference betwen man and animal will still not be found in this way. The difference can be seen only when we grasp how, in the moment of standing erect, a human being is freeing himself from his connection with the animal at the beginning of his life, and establishing his balance in the whole world. Never during his life would he have been able to acquire the skill for doing this had it not been prepared in the most remote days; the seed for it was already within the being of man during the Saturn-existence. Divine Spirits then laid down the seed of the skill that comes to light when the child learns, as we say, to walk. There were no animals then, for they came later, during the Sun-evolution. Hence the human being, as originally planned, is older than the animals.

All that lies in these invisible forces that enable man to walk leads us back to his origin during the Saturn-existence.

The second faculty arising in the child comes from his new orientation in space; this causes the forces to turn inwards and to appear in a different way. For instance, I take up a piece of chalk; a force comes in an inward direction, discharging itself in the internal organs. This inward-turning force, coming through the limbs from the direction of movement, makes its appearance in the child's development when it learns to speak. First, when the child finds its bearings in space, the forces take an outward direction; the same forces then turn inwards and the child learns to speak.

Science knows only a small part of all this. It knows that a right-handed person has his speech-centre in the left half of the brain, and a left-handed person has it in the right half. Everything in the brain that has to do with the development of speech, however, is first worked into it by the limbs when the child learns to walk, to grasp things, to move around and turn its attention to objects. This springs from the inwardly directed forces, which then go out from the brain into the organs of speech. Here, again, divine-spiritual Beings have been preparing the human organism through countless ages, so that the child should be able to speak. Those divine Beings, who during the Saturn period prepared the human being for walking, then worked during the Sun period to bring about his capacity for speech.

The third gift developed by the child, and by all mankind, through speech—for it could not come before speaking in earthly evolution—was the power to have thoughts. This was prepared by the divine-spiritual Beings during the Moon age. That is how human evolution took its course in the past ages of the world; generations of spiritual Beings have prepared for man his walking, speaking, thinking—through Saturn-evolution, Sun-evolution, Moon-evolution.

In the evolution of the world during the Sun age, animals made their appearance—naturally in a form different from that of to-day. They now have to feed on plants, which at that time they had no need to do, for then they were creatures of the air and consisted of airy substance. It was during the Moon-existence that the plants were added.

Then evolution passed over to Earth-existence, when the human being first developed a visible bodily form in which the forces of walking, speaking and thinking could dwell. At the same time the mineral kingdom arose and became an essential part of his organism. In this way man's past can be described.

If we wish to look at man's future, in the light of present-day conditions on Earth, we must start from his old age, which means describing something that is not at all apparent to-day. When a child begins to walk, speak, think, external signs of this are clear enough, but how the spiritual part of man is intensified in old age is far from evident to anyone without spiritual vision. I spoke of the most wonderful experience of watching the gradual revelation of soul and spirit in the growing body of a young child, and of how, if one sees it in the right way, one can be overwhelmed by the deepest religious feeling in face of all the meaning that this artistic process conveys. But it is also wonderful to see how all that a man has experienced through walking, speaking and thinking during his earthly life disappears into the spiritual. And then to see how his thoughts and words, everything he has worked and struggled for with his hands, is carried back into the life of the spirit when he passes through the gate of death. Just as that which comes to expression in the child's walking, speaking, thinking, points us back to previous stages in the Earth's evolution, to the evolution of Moon, of Sun, of Saturn, so does all that a man has experienced in his thoughts point us first of all to his next earthly life, and then to the great periods in the future evolution of the Earth.

So it is that the thoughts of men point towards the Jupiter stage in the evolution of the world and of man—a stage that can be reached only when the Earth has passed through death and risen to a new planetary existence. For thoughts will not then live in us in their present fluctuating way; they will take definite shape and appear in the very form of man.

To-day we are able to keep our thoughts to ourselves, and on certain occasions our countenance can appear perfectly innocent, although we are inwardly guilty. We shall not be able to do this during the Jupiter-existence. A man's thoughts will then engender the expression of his face. The human form will have lost its mineralised firmness; it will be inwardly flexible and will consist of a quite soft substance. A wrong thought rising up in us will instantly show itself to other people through a change in our expression. Everything in the nature of a thought will at once take shape; a man will then go about in the guise of his own enduring thoughts and temperament. Hence if, during the Jupiter-existence, a man is a regular scoundrel, or has only animal impulses, that is what he will look like. That is the first stage in man's future.

The second stage will exemplify the creative power of speech. To-day speech arises inwardly and is sent out only into the air. In the future, the spoken word will not fade away into the air but will continue to exist, and with it a man will create actual forms. So that in the Jupiter age he will have power to shape himself by his thoughts; in the Venus-existence he will give form to the world around him. If during the Venus-existence—when all substance will be as fine as air—he utters an evil word, something like a repulsive plant-form will come into being. Hence a man will be surrounded by the creations of his own speech. During the Venus existence creative feelings will arise, creative speech, and the feelings that create through the word.

During the last metamorphosis of the Earth, the Vulcan-

THE EVOLUTION OF THE WORLD 179

existence, the activities expressed in our walking and the movements of our arms will develop further. To-day we go to our work and use our arms to carry out actions, but nothing of that is lasting. I go to some place; I have something or other to do. It may of course be something quite complicated—possibly even the waging of war. Then we go away again, and in the outer world none of our actions remain. During the Vulcan-existence, everything will remain. A man will not simply go about and perform actions; everything he does will leave its imprint on the Vulcan-existence. His deeds will be actualised, will become realities.

You see how the Earth-existence makes a radical incision between past and future in the evolution of the world and of man. Everything up to the time of the Earth was brought about by divine generations of the spirit; that which is to follow will be brought about by man himself. That is how freedom enters his life within the cosmos. He is placed into the world by the Gods, and given his free existence. From the Gods he has acquired his capacity for walking, speaking, thinking—even his form; but for the future evolution of the world he will have to bring into this walking, speaking and thinking what he himself is. He is now about to live himself out of the past into the future. Part of the past, it is true, lies in his own karma; part of the future lies in what he is willing to do for his own karma in the future. At present he is serving a kind of apprenticeship between past and future.

All this means that things cannot work out in exact conformity with the originally-intended plan I referred to yesterday. I spoke then of 2,160 years having to pass between two incarnations. But during his earthly life a man is far from absorbing all that he could absorb; hence for many people to-day the interval between death and a new birth proves to have changed—no longer 2,160 years for anyone, but essentially shorter.

Men who have given themselves up entirely to an earthly life, those with certain criminal tendencies, are very poorly equipped for sailing out into the ocean of starry existence; and after a short time between death and rebirth they very soon return to earthly life. Others need a long time in which to purify and perfect what they have made of their soul and spirit during life on Earth. So one can say that those with animal tendencies, who easily succumb to their instincts and desires, soon come back to Earth, while those with a normal spiritual development take longer to return. But there may also be human beings who, through a deeper insight during earthly life into the way things are going at the present time, are able to arouse in themselves a self-sacrificing wish to return as soon as possible in order to contribute to the future course of earthly affairs. For if a man has filled his spirit with love during his life on Earth, he can make the three to six transits, through Mars, Jupiter and Saturn, more quickly. When persons with lower instincts pass through death, they draw back trembling before these circles and do not complete them; they are particularly repelled by the region of the planetoids. To-morrow I shall be speaking of how human beings to-day are enabled to enter various circles by sub-mitting themselves to certain influences in the world, in their personal life, in their national life, and so on.

Those who enter the region of the planetoids rightly will to-day spend seven or eight hundred years between one earthly life and the next. That is normal for people who are not of an actually degraded nature. But through deeper insight into things, and through love of the spiritual world, life between death and a new birth can be consciously shortened. Those who have gained much from their life on Earth can make a comparatively quick return, so that as soon as possible they can work on the transforming of earthly civilisation and culture.

I have had to take you in thought away from the earthly world into that of the stars and their inhabitants, so that, in a way suited to the present time, your attention may be directed away from the world in which human beings are generally engrossed, to a world they have to enter through deeper knowledge, if they wish to experience their future aright. To-day, people in general are little inclined to detach themselves from the claims of the material world and to seek the spiritual directly in the physical world around them. We have no time now to dwell on the obstacles met with when, in psycho-analysis, for example—to which I shall be referring to-morrow—attempts are made to investigate at least the spiritual part of man. It is, however, precisely from observing directly the sense-perceptible that a right path will open out for those who wish now to work entirely within the field of present-day science, if they really seek to discover the spiritual there. It can be done. Definite proof of this is to be found in the booklet just issued by our Institute of Physiology and Biology at Stuttgart. Here Frau Dr. Kolisko has published the results of a beautiful piece of research under the title *Physiological and Physical Proof of the Efficacy of the smallest Entities.** You know how homeopathy likes to work with highly diluted substances. By this means, by bringing physical substance in a highly diluted form, a way is opened into the spiritual. Frau Dr. Kolisko has now succeeded in showing, by an exact method, that the smallest entities, the highest dilutions, are effective. She has been working most conscientiously for a long time on the lines I have indicated, and she has now succeeded in producing dilutions in the proportion 1 : 1 trillion.

If any substance is completely dissolved in a glass of water, half of which is then thrown out and the remaining half poured into a full glass of water, we get a dilution of 1 : 2. When half the water is again thrown out and the remainder poured into a full glass, we get 1 : 4, and so on. Now in our Biological Institute at Stuttgart, by means of exact scientific methods, a way has been found to produce precise solutions of 1 : 1 trillion—thus arriving at the so-called higher potencies. The results can be seen in the case, let us say, of anti-

---

* Contained in *Agriculture of Tomorrow* by E. and L. Kolisko, Kolisko Archive Publications, Bournemouth 1978 (Ed.).

mony, about which I spoke in the medical lecture given during our days here. We find that plant growth, for example, the growth of a grain of wheat, is reduced to its slowest rate at about the twenty-first potency, and brought to its fastest rate at about the twenty-ninth or thirtieth potency. So, you see, a substance has been diluted in fluid to a high potency, and we find that the lower potencies have a different effect upon plant growth while the highest potencies accelerate growth, which means that they give the greatest stimulus to the life-force. In this way it has been found possible to break down the purely material, so that the spiritual can manifest there. For if you split up material substance, not into atoms as atomists would have it, but in such a way as to bring out the activity of its functions and forces, then you are showing willingness, I would say, to go over to the spiritual by permeating matter itself with spirit.

You can imagine now what this means for observing accurately how remedies work on the human organism, for the effect can indeed be seen. The dilution is prepared; you have it in a laboratory flask, and you drop into this potency a grain of wheat; then into the potency in the next flask you drop another grain, and so on—grains and grains of wheat. For in the course of this exact research whole rooms were filled with these germinating grains, showing the effect of each potency on the soil out of which the grains sprout. That is what must be done in science to-day, in order to drive material knowledge on into the realm of the spirit. You know what contention there has been between homoeopaths and allopaths concerning the effectiveness of the smallest entities in the higher potencies. The whole affair up to now has been a question of opinion—the allopaths holding to one view, the homoeopaths to another. Here, however, it is not a case of siding with homoeopaths, but of establishing scientifically the actual facts. In the future it will naturally be known when remedies should be applied in the direct allopathic way, and when in a dilution of the correct potency, so that they may have the desired effect on the patient—particularly on his etheric body, which represents the life-forces. We shall know exactly where to draw the line—here you must give an allopathic treatment, there a homoeopathic one. For just as other scientific experiments are carried out with the utmost exactitude, so in this case Frau Dr. Kolisko has shown in her booklet, with the same exactitude, how the smallest entities really work. What was formerly mere surmise has been raised to the level of an important scientific subject.

But all this points to something further. Just look in this booklet at the accurately worked-out curves which show how the forces of growth go up and down; notice how the curves have to be drawn according to whether the potency is strong or weak, how with certain dilutions there is a minimum of growth, and in more dilute solutions—higher potencies—a maximum; then a return to the minimum, back again to the maximum—and so on. Thus, in the remarkably conscientious tracing of the curves, one gains direct insight into a rhythm working in everything material—a rhythm that is indeed the expression of the spiritual. With human beings, we can turn from the metabolic system to the rhythmical system; it is possible in nature, also, to find in a quite exact, scientific way its rhythmical system. That is precisely what is to be seen in this work, which I believe may prove to be an important landmark, not only in the controversy between homoeopathy and allopathy but in all questions concerning our insight into nature. If the results of this research are estimated rightly, the laws of nature in future will no longer be sought only in the present atomistic way, by measuring and weighing; it will be recognised how in all material things there is a rhythm, and how in the rhythm of events in nature the rhythm of the cosmos is expressed.

I wanted to draw your attention to this as a way leading out from exact science that must be opened up. To-morrow I will go on to show how in psycho-analysis, for example, there is a kind of theoretical aversion towards any real setting out on the path leading from physical nature to the spiritual. But if men are to go forward and not backward in civilisation, they will be obliged to take this path to the spirit.

XIII

The Entry of Man into the Era of Freedom

From the descriptions given yesterday you will have gathered that man has gradually to acquire freedom in the present period of world and human evolution. On looking back into the past evolution of the world, we find how, in respect of his most important activities, his walking, speaking, thinking, man has been prepared from above by divine-spiritual Beings. We see how, in order to ensure that what these divine Beings have accomplished in man during his earthly existence shall take effect, if only unconsciously, he is always led between death and rebirth into association with these Beings.

You will remember that I spoke of a man being led through the forces of Sun and Moon, and then, in the realm of the Sun, through Mars, Jupiter, Saturn, into the world of the stars, spiritually understood. To this I would add that when a man in the life between death and rebirth has, so to say, to retrace his steps after, as at present, progressing in the region of the planetoids to a perception of the Saturn impulses, on this return journey he comes into relation with the most sublime divine-spiritual Beings of the higher Hierarchies— Thrones, Cherubim, Seraphim. These are spiritual Beings whose impulses extend over both spiritual and natural existence. While entering into the laws of nature and infusing them with life and with spirit, they have the purpose of bringing about enduring harmony between these laws of nature and the moral life of the whole Cosmos. They are Beings who have never appeared in any physical form, yet in the spiritual world they exercise a scarcely conceivable power upon the Earth, and make it possible for moral law to be brought into continuous harmony with natural law. And so, because a man during his existence beyond the Earth is able constantly to give new life to impulses of the past, he reaches a point in his evolution when he can work in accordance with these extra-earthly impulses.

In the present epoch of the evolution of world and of man, however, we are faced with the task of taking under our own free control everything that in the past was more or less a matter of compulsion, determined for all human beings by higher Powers.

When we survey this evolution of world and of man we find that at a certain definite time man encountered difficulties which had to be overcome on his way from being led exclusively by divine-spiritual Beings to the conscious work of raising himself to knowledge of these Beings and so to the gaining of human freedom. This point of time, which in a certain sense signifies the greatest crisis in the whole evolution of man, came approximately 333 years after the Mystery of Golgotha. Such dates are only approximate owing to time being reckoned in various ways. According to our present reckoning, it was 333 years after the Mystery of Golgotha that this crisis came about.

If we look back at this critical moment, we can describe it more or less in the following way. If the evolution of mankind and that of the Earth itself had continued as they were doing, if men had remained under the guidance of the divine-spiritual Beings who had been leading them up to that time, then, since it was intended by those Beings that men should acquire freedom, it would have been achieved—but with what result? At that time it would have meant upsetting the balance between the two parts of the human astral body.

Think of the connection between the physical body and the astral body : we will keep to the astral body first. Before the year 333 the greater part of the astral body had been active essentially in the upper man, and its smaller part in his lower body—the middle man being between the two. And because in those times the upper part of the astral body was the more powerful, it was through it that divine-spiritual Beings exercised upon man their greatest influence. In accordance with the plan for mankind, human evolution has proceeded in such a way that up to about 3,000 years before Christ those conditions for the astral body held good, but by 1,000 years before Christ the lower part of the astral body was becoming larger and the upper part relatively smaller, until, in the year 333, the two parts had become equal. This was the critical situation 333 years after the coming of Christ, and since then the upper part of a man's astral body has been continuously decreasing. That is the course taken by his evolution.

It is impossible to follow the evolution of man in its reality unless we are able to understand what happens to the human astral body in the course of earthly evolution. If human beings had not undergone this decrease in the upper part of the astral body, their Ego would never have been able to gain sufficient influence and they could never have become free. This decrease in the astral body therefore contributes to the evoking of freedom. I have already said that there is no sense in asking why the Gods have not arranged everything to give human beings pleasure. The Gods had to create a universe that was inherently possible. Much that gives men the greatest pleasure rests on that, besides other things which, until they are enlightened, they do not find at all agreeable. This decrease of the astral body is connected with something else, for on the size of the astral body in the upper part of man—not on its size as a whole—depends his power to control, with his Ego and astral body, his physical and etheric bodies. Hence all men are likely to have their health gradually impaired by this decrease in the astral body. We can form a true conception of human evolution only if we recognise that freedom has to be paid for on Earth by a general weakening of health. Not, of course, in the form of cholera or typhus, but freedom is not to be gained without bringing ill-health of some kind along with it.

If all human forces after the year 333 had remained as they were, men on Earth would have become weaker and weaker, increasingly powerless. And earthly life would have come to an end through this complete decadence of mankind.

At this point there took place what I should like to describe as follows. At a gathering of those divine-spiritual Beings I spoke of as belonging to the Sun, it was decided to send down to the Earth their representative, the Christ, there to go through something that the divine Beings connected with mankind would be experiencing for the first time. Birth and death are certainly not what materialists imagine them to be, but they are part of man's earthly existence. None of the divine-spiritual Beings above man—Angels, Archangels, and so on up to the highest—had ever known death, but only metamorphoses. They change from one form to another, but they are not born and do not die. A man, too, changes form, but at the same time he lays aside his physical and etheric bodies, thus making birth and death a more radical change than any change experienced by the higher Hierarchies. So the leaders in the harmonies and impulses of the Sun resolved to send down to Earth the Christ, as a Being who had not yet experienced birth and death, so that He might go through this purely human destiny. The Mystery of Golgotha, therefore, is not merely the concern of mankind; it is also a concern of the Gods, and this can be put into words such as these : The Sun Gods met and held counsel together as to the steps they should take for warding off from mankind the danger of becoming weaker and weaker through the decline of the astral body.

And so the Christ was sent down to Earth and went through birth and death—naturally not as a human being but as a divine Being. The consequence was that through the Mystery of Golgotha, through the fact of Christ's death, forces came into Earth-evolution for the healing of those other forces which, in the sense already described, were the cause of sickness. Thus Christ became for mankind, in very truth, the great cosmic and terrestrial Healer of mankind. In other words, His forces entered everything that has to be healed in human beings, so that man, having his tendency to decadence on the one hand, but on the other the saving forces of Christ, can find his way to freedom. Therefore, provision was made in world-evolution to ensure that, 333 years before the great crisis, the Mystery of Golgotha should take place.

Human evolution on Earth, accordingly, could not have gone forward without this threat of disastrous universal sickness, to begin in the year 333. Then, through the Mystery of Golgotha, came the great universal healing. Everything therefore done by man without Ego-consciousness, everything that derives from the deeper forces tending to his future downfall, can be healed through association with the Christ. That is what the Mystery of Golgotha means for earthly and human evolution.

The situation I have just been explaining was known, until the fourth century after the coming of Christ, to certain men who still had some knowledge of the facts through having absorbed the spiritual life of their time. In all ages before the Mystery of Golgotha there had been old Mysteries, where the pupils were instructed concerning men's past earthly evolution, the coming of Christ, and what was to take place in mankind's future evolution. They were shown in great and powerful pictures the connection of men on Earth with the spiritual Beings of the higher worlds. At the time of the Mystery of Golgotha there were still isolated individuals here and there who, though scarcely more advanced than the old Mystery pupils, had preserved some knowledge of these matters—a knowledge later called Gnosis. They were scattered through Western Asia, Africa, Southern Europe. Their knowledge, their wisdom, extended to the source of events in the evolution of Earth and man, and to the mighty part played by the Mystery of Golgotha for dwellers on the Earth. But these men, who still had knowledge of the old Mystery secrets, were filled with anxiety. They knew that a crisis was coming for mankind. They knew that in the future human understanding would no longer be able to fathom the depths of earthly and human evolution.

Thus, in certain personalities of the first four Christian centuries it is possible to discern anxiety—not about earthly affairs but about the whole course of world-evolution. Will men be truly ripe enough, they asked, to receive what the Mystery of Golgotha has brought? This, in the first four centuries after the Mystery of Golgotha, was the great question for those we might call successors of the old Initiates.

From among those who in these first centuries were still initiated in Christian Mysteries there came, for example, a wonderful poem. It told of the coming of Christ to Earth, but it also gave in impressive dramatic form—although as a whole the poem was epic—powerful pictures of the men of the near future, who would no longer be able to understand the need for a healing element in human evolution. After these pictures had revealed something of what the Gods had decreed from the Sun—in the way I mentioned—and the descent of Christ into the man Jesus had been impressively described, the poem went on to picture how in human evolution there was to be, in a new, metamorphosed form, a revitalising of the old Demeter-Isis being. It was shown how this being was to be revered in a special, powerfully depicted human form, coming in the future as a solemn promise to mankind.

These poet-priests, as I might call them, of the first four Christian centuries, or at least the most outstanding among them, described how in the further evolution a certain cult was to arise, practised by all who were to attain to learning and a life of the spirit. For such men a sacrificial act of some kind would be established.

The epic pictured a younger man who was to enter into the whole way in which human evolution at that time was understood. It was shown how he was to pass from youth to maturity by developing a cult of the Virgin. This ritual observance, this sacrificial act, shown as necessary for all who were becoming learned and wise, if humanity was to find connection with what had come to men through the Mystery of Golgotha, was portrayed in vivid colours. A mighty poem, full of colour, came into being in those early centuries of Christianity. And among those living more or less in the atmosphere of this poem there were also painter-priests, who, it is true, painted these scenes in the simple way understood by ordinary folk; but their pictures had power and went straight to the heart.

This is what that poem accomplished. But together with all that came definitely from the Gnosis, it was rooted out later by the Church. We have only to remember how it was merely by so-called chance that later on the writings of Scotus Erigena were saved, and it will not seem absurd when spiritual research claims that this greatest of poems, evoking the New Testament, was exterminated root and branch by the later Church, so that nothing of it was left in the following centuries. Yet this poem had been there. It was rooted out, together with all the simple but impressive paintings connected with it. Concealed in it was all the anxiety felt at the time by the successors of the old Initiates. There rang through this poem the grave tones of an elegy.

Now, among those who did not follow Augustine into a quite different stream, a number of people retained the capacity to understand these things right into the fourth century, even up to the beginning of the fifth. But this understanding could not remain as vivid as it had once been; the spiritual forces of people in Southern Europe were no longer adequate for that. So the fundamentals of understanding became crystallised in the dogmas that have endured, though this could not have happened if the dogmas had not been preserved in a language growing ever more lifeless—the Latin language. This carrying on of Latin into the Middle Ages by learned men had the effect of benumbing a once living understanding, so that finally all that was known about Christ becoming man, about the sending of the Spirit, and about the great healing of which I have spoken, had become rigidified in dogmas. These dogmas were propagated through the Latin tongue, the very words of which had nothing more to do with the true content of the teaching. Thus, in the spreading of Western scholarship through the medium of Latin, there took place a gradual drying-up of the fiery, phosphoric element which had permeated that exterminated poem.

Then came all the youthful peoples of the North, stirred up more from the East, and they received the Christ Impulse in the latinised form through which it was losing vitality.

We must picture this Christ Impulse coming up from the South, and the peoples who spread over the North accepting a dried-up Christianity because their youthful spiritual forces lacked power to give fresh life to the greatness underlying the frozen dogmas. The aftermath of all this is still with us to-day. Even now in those Northern regions there can apparently be found—for all this is only apparent—forces that seem to have been too late in receiving the Christ Impulse, already rigid in dogma, but are called upon, out of direct knowledge of the spirit, to rediscover all the secrets of the fact of Golgotha and of Christ's entry into earthly life—all of which has, however, to be re-discovered in complete freedom. For even the fact that after the year 333, Christianity, in its benumbed state, made its way up out of Italy, and young races of men swept down, whose successors are now spread throughout Russia, Sweden, Norway, Middle Europe, England, still living under that same influence—all this came about so that, ultimately, human beings should be able to lay hold of the Christ Impulse in freedom.

It is the present task of those peoples who, as representatives of a civilisation, are the first to whom Anthroposophy has to be brought, to accept all that is connected with Christ Jesus, and to recognise that without the Christ Impulse all men would have become mere "pillars of salt". We can use these physical terms, for the Christ Impulse goes into the physical—right into the healing of the physical. Christ has become the great spiritual Phosphorus working to overcome the salt-forming processes in man. *Christus verus Phosphorus* —this phrase could be heard on all sides in the first three centuries of Christianity. It was also a leading motif in the lost poem I have described.

So, between past and future, we must take our place in the present, and by the same token be able to look back. Naturally, I have no wish to urge upon you dogmatically what I have just been relating about a lost poem and a forgotten teaching. That is far from my intention. But the methods leading to investigation of man's true spiritual course bring us knowledge of such facts, no less reliable than the facts discovered by modern science and far more reliable than its hypotheses. Just as nobody can be compelled to interest himself in matters which, influenced by present-day materialism, he has always rejected, so will nobody who is as sure of them as of his own life be deterred from speaking of them to those who, with a sound feeling for the whole course of human evolution, are able to perceive the reality of such an impulse at work therein.

After the fourth century of Christianity, the poem referred to no longer existed, but in certain circles many details of it were passed on by word of mouth, and lived on in memory. But the members of these circles were prevented by the growing power of the Church from speaking publicly of any such occurrences during the early Christian centuries. One of those who still had some notion of the poem—though they knew of it only in a greatly changed and weakened form—and some idea of the mood from which it arose, was the teacher of Dante. It may indeed be said that Dante's *Commedia,* though dogmatically inclined, owed some of its inspiration to what had been there in the first few Christian centuries.

Naturally I am well aware of the objections that can be made to such an interpretation of history—I could make them myself. But recognising, as one must, the care taken by authors of the history taught in our schools, and with all respect for the precision that relies on records and conscientious historical criticism, what is it all worth? It cannot claim to be true history, real history, for it takes no account of those records which have been side-tracked in the course of time. Hence, though documents may be subjected to the most conscientious criticism, true history will be revealed only in the same way as true knowledge of nature and of the heavens—through spiritual investigation. Men must therefore find courage not only to speak about the world of the stars, as we have been doing during our time here, but also to introduce into the usual presentation of history all that it lacks because it was in the interest of certain circles to deprive posterity of relevant documents. But the impulses in those destroyed documents live on in the souls of human beings; live on in those who have come later and crave for the impulses no longer recorded but once so alive in mankind. Hence it will not only be necessary for men—if they wish to reach in their evolution the future intended for them—to transform, to a certain extent, many of their concepts; they will have also to transform their attitude to the truth.

To speak fundamentally: we must find our way again to Christ. Christ *must* come again. This assumes that during the present century there will be men able to understand in what way Christ will announce His presence, in what guise He will appear. Otherwise terrible disturbances may be stirred up by people who, having in the subconscious depths of their being a premonition of this coming of Christ in the spirit, will represent it to others in a shockingly superficial way. Clear vision into man's evolution during the early future will be possible only when an ever-increasing number of people are sufficiently ripe to see how spiritual research can make real progress; people who are able to discover in the spiritual world what men need for the right shaping of their further course. Failing this, we shall become more and more implicated in all that hinders our approach to the spiritual—not so much where ideas and concepts are concerned, as in our general attitude.

In the ideas and concepts of to-day there is much which looks like a movement towards what must be the true goal of knowledge in our time. In fact, however, this serves somewhat to hinder men from seeing the findings of natural science in the right light. They are left groping for the facts, as it were, in the dark. Observe how to-day—with the general spreading of scientific, medical conceptions—we hear of men who in their later life begin to suffer from nervous troubles that affect their whole physical constitution and lead to genuine symptoms of illness. Our present-day physicians realise, then, how powerless they are to get the better of these symptoms in any obvious way, or to proceed from pathology to therapy. As an immediate contemporary of the outstanding Viennese physician, Breuer, I remember his having a patient in whom physical examination could detect no pathological condition. It was decided to have recourse to hypnosis, which was becoming very popular at that time. Under hypnosis, the patient was found to have had, at an earlier period in his life, a terrible experience, overwhelming him with horror. As far as could be made out, this experience had been repressed into the realm of the subconscious, the unconscious, creating there a "hidden province" of the soul. Though the man himself knew nothing of this, it was there in his life and threatened his health. A man can thus have within him something which, beginning as a soul-experience, has disturbing after-effects; it sets up in his soul an isolated region of which he is unconscious.

It was thought that if the patient recalled his experience, and so became fully conscious of it, this very awareness would lead to his cure.

Cases such as this will be found with increasing frequency in life to-day. But if we are to understand why people are afflicted so often in this way, spiritual knowledge must teach us what happens when the upper part of the astral body decreases, while in its lower part there is a tendency to accumulate subconscious provinces of the soul. We must rise from knowledge of man's soul to the historical knowledge of the spirit, to cosmic spirit-knowledge, in order to explain such phenomena. I knew Breuer well; he was a man of depth; and, because he felt that with our present degree of knowledge no progress was to be made in these matters, he gave up this line of research. He then became involved with other interests, particularly with those of Freud and his followers. Out of that grew psycho-analysis, which rests upon something true, for the phenomena certainly exist. The origin of physical symptoms must be searched for in the soul; the idea is quite right. But the knowledge needed to master the phenomena is not to be found here, for it has to become spiritual knowledge.

Hence this psycho-analysis, which has to do with the quite natural, historical decrease in man's upper astral body, is in the hands of people who are not only amateurs at investigating soul and spirit, but also amateurs in the investigation of the physical body, not knowing how to follow the working of spirit there. So we have two forms of dilettantism coming together; they are really alike, for these people know just as little of the real life of man's soul and spirit as they do of his physical and etheric life. The two extents to which they are dilettante coincide; and when two similar quantities work on each other, they multiply: $a \times a = a^2$, or $d \times d = d^2$; thus dilettantism $\times$ dilettantism $=$ dilettantism squared. So it really comes about that something right, based on true foundations, appears amateurish because of the weakness of present-day research. In all this, however, we can see a striving in the right direction. Anything like psycho-analysis should not, therefore, be treated as an invention of the devil, but as an indication that this age of ours wants something it is unable to achieve, and that anything like psycho-analysis will prosper only when founded on spiritual research. Otherwise psycho-analysis will come to us in the strange form to which Jung's logic has driven it.

Jung is indeed capable of writing, for example, a sentence such as this: One can say that through the "hidden provinces" of the soul, man was at one time disposed to assume the existence of a Divine Being. Jung then adds (he is, of course, inclined to atheism): It is obvious that such a Being cannot exist. Psycho-analysis, however, argues that man, having this disposition to believe, must assume the existence of a Divine Being in order to preserve the balance of his soul. For a conscientious person—and I would never fail to recognise that a man such as Jung is both conscientious and precise—this really means: You are obliged to live with an untruth because you are unable to live with the truth. There is no truth in theism, but you have to live with it. In our state of development to-day such things are not taken in earnest; they must, however, be taken with all possible earnestness.

So on all sides, without it being realised, these subconscious yearnings arise. Those of you who have heard or read other lecture-cycles of mine will know that I have often pointed out, from spiritual perception, how it is not right to say: Light streaming from the Sun, for example, goes out endlessly into the infinity of cosmic space, always decreasing in intensity with the square of the distance.

I have repeatedly said that spiritual perception gives a different picture. The idea that light from a centre streams out into endless distance is not correct. Just as a bow-string when drawn can be stretched only to a certain point, and will then spring back, so light goes only to a certain point and always returns. It does not only expand; it is also elastic, rhythmical. Hence the Sun not only radiates light but is all the while receiving it back; for at the end of their outward course the intensity of the rays is different and their course can be changed. I want merely to indicate this as revealing itself in connection with higher cognition, with cosmic knowledge of the world—the true knowledge of Spiritual Science.

Please do not take these remarks as indicating any lack of respect for science on my part. I appreciate science fully; it cannot be sufficiently praised, and one must recognise the high level of intelligence it brings into life to-day. But its statements about light, for example, are amateurish compared with the truth. It is important that the truth should be reached, if only to bring into all these prevailing ideas, which men do not know how to deal with, the impulse that could raise present-day research into the spiritual realm.

In certain occult circles there is a wrong practice : the student is given various occult teachings, but is never brought to the point of being shown whence they derive. The teachings are given in pictures, and the student is not led on to the realities which are imaged in the pictures. Hence his soul is surrounded by a world of pictures, and he never comes to see that through the pictures he ought to be learning about the whole Cosmos.

For this reason, after my *Theosophy* had appeared, it had to be followed by *Occult Science*. Here the pictures given in *Theosophy* are led on into the reality of the starry world, into the evolution of the Earth through Saturn, Sun, Moon, and so on. The two books are complementary to each other.

When in any sphere men are given nothing but pictures, they are hemmed in by them. Persons who practise a wrong kind of occultism do this with a student they are not sure of, and by this means they lead him into what is called "occult imprisonment". He is then encircled by confusing pictures from which there is no escape—a veritable prison of pictures. That is how much occult harm has been practised, and is still practised to-day. There are even spiritual beings who drive certain people into this occult captivity; but for the soul the phenomenon is just the same. These spiritual beings are let loose in nature when nature is not understood spiritually, but viewed as though atomic processes were part of nature. The spirit in nature is thus denied. Those spirits who are always striving to work against man—the Ahrimanic spirits—then become active in nature, encompassing man with pictures of every kind, so that in this case, too, human beings are occultly imprisoned.

A great part of what to-day is called the scientific outlook— not the facts of science, for they can be relied on—consists of nothing else than pictures of the general occult captivity threatening to overtake mankind. The danger lies in the surrounding of people everywhere with atomistic and molecular pictures. It is impossible, when surrounded by such pictures, to look at those of the free spirit and the stars; for the atomistic picture of the world is like a wall around man's soul—the spiritual wall of a prison house.

This prospect can show us, in the light of Spiritual Science, what should be rightly striven for to-day. The facts of natural science are always fruitful and lead out into the wide realms of the spirit, if they are not approached with the prejudices of the occult prison in which, fundamentally, science is at present confined. These things must be a deep inward experience for us, if we wish to take our right place in the evolution of the Earth and mankind, in accordance with its past and its future. It is all this that speaks to us when in some region we have before our eyes the evidence of human aspiration in the past and are now able to see it in the full light of spirit and of soul.

When here we climb the hills and come upon the Druid stones, which are monuments to the spiritual aspirations of those ancient times, it can be a warning to us that the longings of those people of old who strove after the spirit, and looked in their own way for the coming Christ, will meet with fulfilment only when we, once again, have knowledge of the spirit, through the spiritual vision that is our way of looking for His coming. Christ must come again. Only thus can mankind learn to know Him in His spiritual form, as once, in bodily form, He went through the Mystery of Golgotha.

This is something that here, where such noble monuments of the past have been preserved, can be felt in a particularly living way.

Recommended for further reading

Occult Science—An Outline Rudolf Steiner
Rudolf Steiner Press, London 1979

The Riddles of Philosophy Rudolf Steiner
Anthroposophic Press, New York 1973

The Christ Impulse and the Development of Ego Consciousness Rudolf Steiner
Steiner Book Centre, Vancouver 1979

Ancient Myths. Their Meaning and Connection with Evolution Rudolf Steiner
Steiner Book Centre, Vancouver 1978

The Effects of Spiritual Development Rudolf Steiner
Rudolf Steiner Press, London 1978

Man: Hieroglyph of the Universe Rudolf Steiner
Rudolf Steiner Press, London 1972

A Road to Self Knowledge Rudolf Steiner
Rudolf Steiner Press, London 1975

Karmic Relationships, Volumes I to VIII
Rudolf Steiner
Rudolf Steiner Press, London 1972–77

Three Streams in the Evolution of Mankind
Rudolf Steiner
Rudolf Steiner Press, London 1965

From Buddha to Christ Rudolf Steiner
Anthroposophic Press, New York 1978

The Spiritual Guidance of Man and Humanity
Rudolf Steiner
Anthroposophic Press, New York 1970

Man and World in the Light of Anthroposophy
Stewart C. Easton
Anthroposophic Press, New York 1975

For Freedom Destined Franz E. Winkler
Waldorf Press, New York 1974

Pharos
paperback series

THE PHILOSOPHY OF FREEDOM
A basis for a modern world conception
Rudolf Steiner
272pp. ISBN 0 85440 350 7

OCCULT SCIENCE
An Outline
Rudolf Steiner
352pp. ISBN 0 85440 349 3

LIVING WITH YOUR BODY
Walther Bühler M.D.
128pp. ISBN 0 85440 345 0

THE WAY OF A CHILD
A.C. Harwood
144pp. ISBN 0 85440 352 3

RUDOLF STEINER EDUCATION
The Waldorf Schools
Francis Edmunds
144pp. ISBN 0 85440 344 2

THE EVOLUTION OF CONSCIOUSNESS
Rudolf Steiner
208pp. ISBN 0 85440 351 5

PHASES
Crisis and Development in the Individual
Bernard Lievegoed M.D.
256pp. ISBN 0 85440 353 1

Further titles in preparation.

THE
PHILOSOPHY OF FREEDOM
Rudolf Steiner

How philosophy as an art is related to human freedom, what freedom is, and whether we do, or can, participate in it — this is the main theme of my book. All other scientific discussions are included only because they ultimately throw light on these questions, which are, in my opinion, the most immediate concern of mankind. These pages offer a Philosophy of Freedom.

All science would be nothing but the satisfaction of idle curiosity did it not strive to raise the value of existence for the personality of man. The sciences attain their true value only by showing the human significance of their results. The ultimate aim of the individual can never be the cultivation of a single faculty, but rather the development of all the capacities that are within us. Knowledge has value only in so far as it contributes to the all-round development of the whole nature of man.

This book, therefore, conceives the relationship between science and life, not in such a way that man must bow down before an idea and devote his powers to its service, but in the sense that he masters the world of ideas in order to use them for his human aims, which transcend those of mere science.

One must be able to confront an idea and experience it; otherwise one will fall into its bondage.

PHASES
Crisis and Development in the Individual
Bernard Lievegoed

Through popular scientific writing and through the media of radio and television, many people have been brought into contact with frequently contradictory views of human nature put forward by different schools of thought in psychology and psychiatry . . .

In this work I have tried to create order in this chaos of conflicting ideas, so that man is seen as a physical being: the biological image of man; as a psyche: the psychological image of man; and as a spirit being: the biographical image of man. The path of an individual's life, his biography, can only be appreciated fully as a unique personal 'work of art' if these three viewpoints are combined to form a single image.

This book gives a general account of the phases in a human being's life, and the characteristic, ever-changing problems and opportunities which they bring. At the same time, certain critical stages and situations in people's lives are discussed along with the problems associated with them. In this way it is hoped that this book will offer the reader a basis for insight into the course of his own life and an understanding of the biographical development of others.

OCCULT SCIENCE
An Outline
Rudolf Steiner

All Occult Science must spring from two thoughts. First that there is, behind the visible, an invisible world hidden to begin with from the senses and from the kind of thinking that is bound to the senses. And secondly that by the development of forces asleep within him it is possible for man to penetrate into this hidden world . . .

The path to Occult Science can be found in due time by all those who perceive — or even only divine or surmise — in the manifest the presence of a hidden aspect. Aware that their powers of knowledge are capable of evolution, they will begin to feel that the hidden can become manifest in them.

THE WAY OF A CHILD
A.C. Harwood

The fact that boredom can be spoken of at all in connection with little children is a sad reflection on our times. It shows that under modern conditions the living world of childhood phantasy, the source of creative imagination in later years, is threatening to dry up. We seem to be losing sight of these relationships, or possibly prefer to ignore them. How strangely anomalous that sophisticated adults have now to be trained to teach little children how to play! Ingenious methods are devised for holding a child's attention, clever toys for play-learning, but still for learning, not living. Are we in danger of losing track of childhood altogether?

LIVING WITH YOUR BODY
Walther Bühler M.D.

Only by looking at man as a total being, composed of body, soul and spirit, is it possible to gain a comprehensive idea of his nature and thus learn to understand more about the questions of health and illness which are so much a part of our day to day lives. Whole food, healthy living, exercise and relaxation are only some of the answers. Others have to be found through an understanding of the different forces working within us.

RUDOLF STEINER
EDUCATION
The Waldorf Schools

Francis Edmunds

On the whole much of our modern education, so far from helping the situation, has had a general tendency to make things worse. It has resulted in waking children up to adult consciousness at too early an age; it has failed to enrich the soul experience and to nourish the imagination on which so much can be built in adolescence; by segregating children into different schools and 'streams', it has produced in many a terrible sense of frustration and failure; it has narrowed the adolescent's horizon by specialisation just at the time when he wants to feel himself master of the world; it has imprisoned the teacher within an examination syllabus when he most needs to develop and demonstrate his freedom . . .

Part of the purpose of this book is to show that by their very nature Steiner Schools are a living protest against these doctrines and practices.